Breaking Away

The Mises Institute dedicates this volume to all of its generous
Supporters and wishes to thank these, in particular:

Patrons

Abdelhamid Abdou
Mr. and Mrs. J. Ryan Alford
Dr. Thomas T. Amlie
Mr. and Mrs. Michael Asselta
Jordan Ausman
Shawn Bardong
Bryan Lee Briggs
Michael L. Burks
Travis Coursey
Richard Cunniff
Jerry T. Dowell
Gerald Dungee, in Memory of Paul S. Dungee
Bill Eaton
Dennis Edwards
Julian Fondren
Lee Friday
Charles F. Hanes
Mr. and Mrs. Jeffrey Harding
Sheldon Hayer
Dr. Frederic H. Herman
Chris and Erin Hindmarch
Dan Johnson and Randee Laskewitz
Dr. Matthias G. Kelm
Russ Marsden
Ralph Martins
Roy and Sarah McCollum
Kevin Menard
Dr. James W. Mulholland, in Memory of Mary R. Mulholland, R.N.
Plus Minus, Inc.
Patrick Rosenwald, in Honour of Greta Rosenwald
Carlos M. Rossi
Dr. Murray and Florence M. Sabrin
Richard L. Stees, Jr.
Loyd J. Stegent, President, Stegent Equity Advisors, Inc.
Emanuel Mark Strategos
Zachary L. Tatum
Dr. James H. Vernier
Richard D. and Susan Williams

Breaking Away

The Case for Secession, Radical Decentralization, and Smaller Polities

Ryan McMaken

MISESINSTITUTE

AUBURN, ALABAMA

Published 2022 by the Mises Institute

Mises Institute
518 West Magnolia Avenue
Auburn, Alabama 36832
mises.org

ISBN: 978-1-61016-758-1

Contents

Foreword by Carlo Lottieri 7

Preface 11

Introduction: Universal Rights, Locally Enforced 15

Part I: Big States, Small States, and Secession 25

   1. More Choices, More Freedom, Less Monopoly Power 27

   2. Political Anarchy Is How the West Got Rich 35

   3. Why Regimes Prefer Big States and Centralized Power 43

   4. Why the Classical Liberals Wanted Decentralization 53

   5. Secession as a Path to Self-Determination 63

   6. Nationalism as National Liberation:
      Lessons from the End of the Cold War 71

   7. A Brief History of Secession Plebiscites in Europe 77

   8. Why the US Supports Secession for Africans,
      but Not for Americans 83

   9. From Taxes to Trade, More Secession Means
      More Freedom 89

  10. If California Secedes, What Happens to Locals
       Who Opposed Secession? 99

  11. How Small Is Too Small? 105

12. When It Comes to National Defense,
    It's More than Size that Matters 111
13. If America Splits Up, What Happens to the Nukes? 123

Part II: Decentralization and Democracy 139

14. Why "One Man, One Vote" Doesn't Work. 141
15. Democracy Doesn't Work Unless It's Done Locally. 151

**Part III: Lessons from America's Past, and Strategies
    for the Future.** 159

16. How Early Americans Decentralized Military Power 161
17. Before *Roe v. Wade*, Abortion Policy was a State
    and Local Matter 173
18. When Immigration Policy Was Decentralized. 181
19. Why Indian Tribal Sovereignty Is Important. 197
20. Sovereignty for Cities and Counties:
    Decentralizing the American States 205
Postscript
    A Tale of Two Megastates: Why the EU Is Better
    (In Some Ways) than the US 211
Index. 219

Foreword

Classical liberal tradition defends the right of secession on many grounds. One of the main reasons is that the territorial dispersion of power limits political domination much more than formal constitutions do. Small states cannot easily adopt protectionist policies and their political classes are closely controlled by the citizens; in addition, redistribution is more difficult and rulers have more direct information about their own reality. Besides that, nationalism is a nonsense in a tiny jurisdiction of only 30,000 people (as in the case of Liechtenstein). Therefore, if we want to protect our fundamental rights, we need competing small states and the best way to enlarge the market is to multiply the jurisdictions.

In *Breaking Away*, Ryan McMaken takes up and elaborates on a number of libertarian arguments supporting self-government and he draws attention to an issue that is not always examined: that of defense and peace.

In the most glorious times of Dutch history, at the entrance to the port of Amsterdam there was this motto: *Commercium et pax* (trade and peace). Free market, social cooperation, and cultural dialogue always go hand in hand. That is why it is not surprising that in so many protagonists of classical liberal thought—from Montesquieu to Constant, from Cobden to Bastiat—free trade is associated with peace. By consequence, a libertarian defense of local self-government can be supported by a strong emphasis on the idea that processes of political disintegration would make a less conflictual world possible.

Yet for five centuries, the state has derived its legitimacy from the claim to guarantee order and avoid chaos. This thesis, in particular, is central to the philosophy of Thomas Hobbes. Similarly, any process of unification always implies that the territorial dispersion of power would be accompanied by tensions, whereas unifications would guarantee harmony between peoples. For many people, talk of political division would already imply some disharmony and enmity.

On the contrary, against this Kantian idea of a global federation leading to the disappearance of borders, McMaken repeatedly focuses on the link between a peaceful international order and the diffusion of local self-government.

The analysis of sovereignty, territoriality or any other aspect of the modern state could take a lifetime, without achieving an understanding of which of these elements most characterizes this institution. However, it is clear that one must look at the state as a machine aimed at centralizing all decision-making power.

As McMaken points out, the state tends to enlarge: "mega-states are the ideal state." After all, in the early modern age the model of statehood (France) emerged at the end of a process of enlargement that wiped out autonomy and diversity, laying the foundations for a growing homogenization of what had previously been a very linguistically, historically, and culturally articulated and inhomogeneous area.

Today one of the most used arguments in support of unification processes (against any hypothesis of secession of individual American states, against any skepticism toward European unification, and so on) is that only by building very large political entities is it possible to ensure effective defense: against China, Russia or any other state power.

The first objection is that if wars are waged by states, then it is necessary to overcome state logic in order to arrive at a more peaceful world. The more the number of states increases, the less they can really be ascribed to the state model. As Hegel pointed out, in some situations quantity can become quality.

However, the question remains as to how a collection of small entities that are much more respectful of individual rights can counteract large imperialist powers.

Basically many people think that large states are more militarily powerful. Obviously, this is not totally false, but we should compare a large armed state and an alliance of small jurisdictions emerging from the dissolution of big institutions. McMaken's thesis is that the freedom provided by local self-government confers more economic dynamism, better technology, and greater attachment to one's local reality. Moreover, it is not altogether surprising that during the last century great military powers have been in trouble when they have tried to occupy small localities where citizens were prepared to become soldiers to defend their families and homes.

After all, even if historians are still very uncertain about various aspects of those events, the Greek-Persian wars cannot be remembered as an undisputed triumph on the part of the most compact and unitary conglomerate.

In the end, in this contrast between those who believe that one must accept (even reluctantly) to be part of a large state in order to avoid a conquest and those, instead, who believe that even in such a case it is important to understand the advantages of the dispersion of power, we find ourselves faced with that misunderstood trade-off between freedom and security. And so it is always worth remembering the lesson of Benjamin Franklin, who was convinced that "those who would give up essential Liberty, to purchase a little temporary Safety, deserve neither Liberty nor Safety."

The problem is that, as the history of large states shows very well, choosing security without freedom leads to losing both rights and peace.

—CARLO LOTTIERI
UNIVERSITY OF VERONA
JULY 2022

Preface

For decades, when American readers have encountered the topics of secession and political decentralization, the discussion has generally been confined to a narrow range of topics around the American Civil War, American constitutional law, and race relations in America.

This book barely mentions any of those things.

Rather, *Breaking Away* differs from countless other books on secession and decentralization in that it considers examples and benefits of secession and radical decentralization in a much broader historical, geographical, and theoretical context. That is, this book isn't necessarily for Americans at all, but for anyone interested in how issues of secession and decentralization come up again and again worldwide as communities of human beings seek self-determination, freedom, and economic prosperity. An examination of these topics also necessitates a look at small states which often only exist because they have successfully resisted efforts at political centralization, or have been formed from successful secession movements of the past. Small states are often the success stories.

Fortunately, scholars in recent decades have begun to focus in greater detail on secession, decentralization, and small states. For many decades, the study of states has focused overwhelmingly on large states and great powers. "State-building" has long been of central interest to many scholars. But the processes of breaking states apart—secession and decentralization—have commanded far less attention.

With this book, I hope to draw upon these new trends in scholarship and expand the typical discussion over secession and decentralization into a larger context. I also present these strategies in terms of general principles that transcend any single nation's history and experience. From local conflicts over social policy to post-colonial secession movements, we can find countless ways in which secession and decentralization have been at the center of national liberation movements and efforts to limit the prerogatives of powerful states.

This book is not intended for academics, however, and in fact has its genesis in many short articles written for a non-academic audience. As such, this book suffers the shortcomings of collections of articles in that some material may be covered more than once here and there, and introductions and conclusions may at times seem abrupt. The up side to this, of course, is that the reader will likely find many of the chapters easy to read in a short amount of time. Moreover, in many places, I have merged chapters and taken steps to create an easier flow.

The book is composed of three sections. The first section looks at numerous historical examples of secession and decentralization as a tactic in dividing up sovereign states into smaller and totally independent states. I also examine the moral, political and practical cases—that is, *not the constitutional or legal cases*—to be made in favor of secession and decentralization. The second section looks at how democratic government institutions function better at a smaller and more localized level. The third section looks at some examples of political decentralization in American history, but with a focus on more obscure examples now largely forgotten or misremembered.

Although there is a philosophical component to this book, it is not primarily theoretical in nature. Rather, it focuses on historical examples and analysis of how secession and decentralization manifest themselves and can be used as tools in the real world. Taken all together, it is my hope that the reader will come away with a better understanding of how political decentralization continues to be relevant, useful, and important in the modern world.

The transformation of vague ideas into the present book was the product of many opportunities and suggestions that came from friends and colleagues. Central to it all is the fact I have been given the opportunity to write at length on these topics for a period of years, and that has been made possible by the tireless work of Lew Rockwell and Jeff Deist in keeping the Mises Institute a place where this sort of research can take place. I'm also thankful for the help and encouragement of my colleagues Tho Bishop and Judy Thommesen who have encouraged me and made the project seem more manageable. The most important factor of all has been my wife and my four children who have been instrumental in forcing me to repeatedly evaluate the ideas here on a practical level. Jessica has always been a source of tireless support and helping to raise four children tends to make one think often of whether or not one's ideas are of any use in making the world a better place in the future. I hope some of the ideas here can help this in some small way.

—Ryan McMaken
Denver, Colorado
June 2022

Introduction:
Universal Rights,
Locally Enforced

The world is now, and has always been, politically decentralized. At no time in history has all of humankind been ruled by a single political regime. Although the Roman Empire claimed to be universal, the Romans never even conquered all of *Europe*, let alone the whole inhabited world. Roman power never extended to India, China, Sub-Saharan Africa, or the Americas. In other words, political power was never wielded from any single place by any single state.

Today, we see decentralization at work in the fact that there are more than two hundred separate sovereign states in the world. Nearly all of them enjoy a sizable amount of political power over their own citizens: imposing taxes, regulating daily life, and exercising police powers. Many of these states command enough military power to compete with other states and exercise true de facto independence even in the international sphere.

In other words, political power in the world is spread across dozens of independent political regimes and national power centers, most of which jealously guard their own powers and prerogatives from other regimes—and from domestic challengers to each state's power.

The decentralization doesn't end there. States themselves are often internally politically decentralized, most obviously in states that employ a federal political structure, such as Switzerland or the United States. Historically, we also find enormous variation in these arrangements. The Holy Roman Empire, for instance, contained more than 1,800 nearly-sovereign subdivisions within its borders during the eighteenth century. In Austria-Hungary in the nineteenth century, political power was divided among a number of internal ethnic, religious, and linguistic groups. The Dutch Republic of the seventeenth century was a confederation of seven self-governing provinces. It was also the most prosperous state of its time.

In these cases of internal decentralization, political power is divided among numerous jurisdictions and sub-national units. Some of these sub-units enjoy a high degree of autonomy. Some do not. But in these cases, political powers are never entirely reserved only to a single national power center.

Thus, we find that *the norm* in human affairs and in human history is a political system that is globally decentralized. It is the norm because most people recognize on an instinctual level that it is impractical—and likely impossible—to fashion a single global polity and regime that can direct all political institutions from a single political center. History suggests that this cannot be done without provoking an endless series of rebellions attempting to implement more local autonomy. Were all of Asia ruled from Tokyo, for example, this regime would be incessantly consumed with the challenges of imposing the regime's will on a culturally and linguistically diverse population spread across millions of square miles. Thus, throughout, human history, the number and size of states in the world frequently changes adjusting to the ability of local interests to achieve autonomy from centers of power, and often to reflect cultural differences from place to place. This reality has not disappeared in our own time, and in many ways it has even accelerated. In fact, since the end of the Second World

War, the number of independent states in the world has nearly tripled.[1]

Secession as a Type of Decentralization

This breaking up of human societies into a number of independent polities and countries is a type of decentralization, and secession is a key tool in this process.

Sometimes states get bigger through state-building processes. But sometimes the opposite happens. When states are broken down into a larger number of relatively smaller states, this is accomplished through secession—the act through which a portion of a state breaks off to create a new state. It's easy to find examples. When the American revolutionaries successfully broke away from the British Empire in the eighteenth century, new states were created, and the borders of the empire were profoundly changed. The Dutch Republic was formed following its secession from the Spanish Empire.

Similarly, as the European colonial powers abandoned—or were forced to abandon—their empires in the nineteenth and twentieth century, new independent states were created. Borders changed and maps were re-drawn.

The same thing happened when the Soviet Union collapsed in the late twentieth century.

So, while the political power in the world is already decentralized to a degree, it could still be decentralized to a far greater extent. The question of further decentralizing political power remains very much a timely topic and an ongoing question.

In 2016, for example, a majority of British voters elected to leave the European Union in favor of maintaining a fully independent and separate British state. In other words, British voters elected to reverse the political centralization that had been growing in the EU's European Commission in Brussels. Two years earlier, in 2014,

---

[1]Alberto Alesina and Enrico Spolaore, "What's Happening to the Number and Size of Nations?" E-International Relations, November 9, 2015, https://www.e-ir.info/2015/11/09/whats-happening-to-the-number-and-size-of-nations/.

Scottish voters went to the polls to vote yes or no on this question: "Should Scotland be an independent country?" At the time, a majority of Scottish voters voted "no" to the proposed separation. The matter is not resolved, however, and the question of Scottish independence continues to be debated both in Scotland and throughout the United Kingdom. Catalonian secessionists in Spain continue to press for a split from Madrid as well.

Political Centralization and the Question of Human Rights

Given the ubiquitous nature of decentralization and secession throughout history, we are faced with an important question: what is the ideal size of a state, and how much of a state's power should reside in the central government? Is it a good thing when a state is broken up into smaller autonomous provinces and regions? Should states be broken up into independent smaller states?

In order to answer these questions, we must first ask by what standard we can judge regimes and political institutions to be "good" or "bad."

For those of us who are adherents of the ideology known as liberalism—also known as "classical" liberalism or libertarianism—the preservation and protection of universal human rights is of exceptional importance, and serves as a central standard by which to judge a regime. At the core of these rights—also known as "natural rights"—are basic freedoms such as the freedom to own private property, freedom of speech, and the freedom to practice one's religion. Only slightly less important in evaluating a regime is the question of ensuring a rising standard of living and preserving conditions for human flourishing.

Why Decentralization Is a Good Thing

The purpose of this book is to illustrate in a variety of ways that decentralization is a good thing and is generally beneficial for the preservation of human rights and economic prosperity. Moreover, it is my position there is not nearly *enough* decentralization. All too often policymakers accept there are at least *some* benefits to decentralization or its cognates such as "subsidiarity" and "federalism." Yet in countless cases, professed respect for principles of decentralization amounts to little more than a token nod in favor of localism. Ultimately, centralized state institutions in these cases end up with the lion's share of political power.[2]

This isn't to say that factors other than the degree of centralization of power are unimportant to matters of human rights and natural rights. For instance, ideology and tradition both play important roles. A population that is ideologically and traditionally inclined toward the protection of universal rights is more likely to live under regimes that respect these rights. This is true regardless of size. All

---

[2]Subsidiarity is a term often used in Catholic and European contexts which is largely synonymous in its usage with "local control," "federalism," or "local sovereignty" in the American context. I will not use the term extensively here, however, because the term is itself imprecise and its meaning is contested among scholars who study subsidiarity. That is, it is no more precise than similar terms like "decentralization" or "localism." Policy prescriptions for a political system adhering to principles of subsidiarity can vary wildly because a commonly accepted definition of subsidiarity is simply that powers should be allocated to the individual or institution that can best or most appropriately exercise them. This is sometimes interpreted to favor giving more power to lower levels of government hierarchy, but not in many cases. Standards for determining what constitutes the best or most appropriate exercise of this power is quite malleable and even those claiming to desire subsidiarity often support further centralization of power because the central authority is in many cases deemed to be the "appropriate" or "best" institution to exercise the power in question. Other standards used to determine whether subsidiarity should favor local control or central control include economic efficiency and justice, but opponents of decentralization need only insist that the central government can deliver more efficiency or more just outcomes. Thus, advocating for subsidiarity (or decentralization) broadly understood, doesn't necessarily advance the position that more decentralization is better. The goal of this book, rather, is to illustrate why *greater* decentralization is desirable—a position that does not necessarily follow from favoring subsidiarity or decentralization in general terms. For more on why subsidiarity is regarded as "vague" and "slippery" see Markus Jachtenfuchs and Nico Krisch, "Subsidiarity in Global Governance," *Law and Contemporary Problems* 79, no. 2 (2016): 5; Andreas Føllesdal, Competing Conceptions of Subsidiarity," *Nomos* 55 (2014): 214–30; Michelle Evans, "The Principles of Subsidiarity as a Social and Political Principle in Catholic Social Teaching," *Solidarity: The Journal of Catholic Social Thought and Secular Ethics* 3, no. 1 (November 2013): 45–46.

else being equal, however, we will find that more political decentralization leads to more responsive, less abusive political institutions.

The benefits of political decentralization can be primarily found in three areas.

One:
Smaller States Allow for More Choice
and More Opportunities for Exit

The first benefit of decentralization is that smaller states and decentralized states allow residents to make more choices as to what sort of regime they wish to live under in order to better meet their needs and protect their rights.

Within the United States, for example, businesses and private citizens move from state to state in order to avoid taxes, regulations, or to otherwise change the nature of the government under which they live.

This occurs at the international level as well, as can be seen in the phenomenon of migrant workers, refugees, asylum-seekers, and businesses all seeking to improve their situations.

Polities that are physically smaller allow for easier relocation and more choice. For example, were the United States composed of just two or three member states, residents would have far fewer choices of governments under which to live. As it is, residents have dozens of choices, at least in terms of policy areas that are not dominated by the federal government.

Similarly, were Europe or South America composed of just one or two sovereign states, residents would have to travel much farther to escape the regimes under which they live. They would also have fewer choices overall.

A large number of independent polities from which to choose also tends to encourage competition among states. In his essay "What We Mean by Decentralization," Lew Rockwell notes:

> under decentralization, jurisdictions must compete for residents and capital, which provides some incentive for greater degrees of freedom, if only because local despotism is neither popular nor

productive. If despots insist on ruling anyway, people and capital will find a way to leave.[3]

Smaller states are less able to monopolize and control the movement, production, and activities of residents when a number of other choices beckon from across the border.

We can put this another way: In the private sector, an industry with a large number of firms offers more choices, and the individual firms themselves possess less monopoly power. The same is true in the "marketplace" of states. More states mean more variety, more choice, and less monopoly power enjoyed by any single state.

Two:
Protecting Minority Rights When Democracy Fails

For centuries, political reformers have sought ways to shape political institutions in ways designed to protect minority groups from being overwhelmed by the majority.

Even in non-democratic political institutions, majority groups tend to exercise far more power than minority groups. This can be magnified in democratic regimes where elections often only serve to solidify policies favored by the majority. Many strategies have been employed to address this problem. Examples include an independent judiciary, and a variety of "checks and balances" designed to allow minority groups a chance to shape policy.

These efforts can often fail if a minority group is unable to win influence in at least some key political institutions. When this happens, minority groups may find themselves as a part of a permanent minority and that means the minority group is locked out of power indefinitely.

When that happens, the only solutions that can be found are in acts outside the realm of institutional political activism. Such acts include boycotts, passive resistance, and armed rebellion. This, of course, can lead to civil war, and it's why secession and decentralization must be

---

[3]Llewellyn H. Rockwell, Jr., "What We Mean by Decentralization," *Mises Daily*, July 21, 2005, https://mises.org/library/what-we-mean-decentralization.

on the table as a means of providing minority groups with a chance at self-determination and self-government.

Three:
Limiting the Power of Aggressive States

A third benefit of decentralization and secession is that they tend to limit the power of regimes and states overall. When regimes seek to increase their own power through conquest, confiscation of property, or other outrages, their potential for damage is limited by the size and scope of the state itself.

According to Rockwell, "tyranny on the local level minimizes damage to the same extent that macro-tyranny maximizes it." That is, "If Hitler had ruled only Berlin, [and] Stalin only Moscow" the history of the world may have been considerably less bloody.[4] Large states are playgrounds for despots and dictators, while small states provide far fewer opportunities for ambitious politicians to spread their mayhem beyond their local communities.

On the whole, small and decentralized states are *less* likely to abuse their power, destroy their economies, and disregard basic human rights. Large, centralized states, on the other hand, are more easily able to abuse their residents and deny their rights, leading also to more dysfunctional economies and diminished economic opportunity.

The end goal of all this secession and decentralization is—to use a phrase employed by the libertarian economist Murray Rothbard— "universal rights, locally enforced." As Rockwell explains, these two concepts—universalism and localism—are frequently in tension. But, he concludes:

> if you give up one of the two principles [i.e., universal rights and local control] you risk giving up liberty. Both are important. Neither should prevail over the other. A local government that violates rights is intolerable. A central government that rules in the name of universal rights is similarly intolerable.[5]

---

[4]Ibid.
[5]Ibid.

States tend to pursue certain goals regardless of size. Regimes want to protect their own prerogatives and ensure the staying power of the state itself. Thus, both large and small states are willing to abuse their powers in pursuit of these goals—*if they can get away with it*. Small and decentralized states, however, face more limitations when it comes to expanding power and limiting the freedoms of taxpayers and residents. It is these de facto limitations on political power that lead to the benefits of decentralization that I will discuss throughout the book.

Part I
Big States, Small States, and Secession

1

More Choices, More Freedom, Less Monopoly Power

Because of their physical size, large states are able to exercise more state-like power than geographically smaller states—and thus exercise a greater deal of control over residents. This is in part because larger states benefit from higher barriers to emigration than smaller states. Large states can therefore better avoid one of the most significant barriers to expanding state power: *the ability of residents to move away.*

The significance of this in practice becomes more clear if we consider the extreme and hypothetical case of a world with a single state. In this case, a person has no other choices at all. The number of actual choices equals zero, since our hypothetical megastate has a monopoly over the entire world. That is, a single global state is the most powerful state possible and a fully-formed state in the strictest sense. It has a complete and total monopoly of force over its population since its citizens cannot escape the state even if they emigrate. There is nowhere that they can emigrate *to*.

On the other hand, a world composed of hundreds, thousands, or even tens of thousands of states (or regimes of varying types) would offer many choices to residents who might wish to change their living situation.

The smaller states become, the more practical relocation options become for residents. This is due to the fact that proximity to the resources and people one desires to be near *does* matter as a real physical constraint. If one can escape a large state's jurisdiction only by emigrating one thousand miles, this is a considerably different situation than in the case of a small state from which exit requires only emigrating fifty miles. In the words of Kirkpatrick Sale, these smaller states are closer to "human scale."[1]

The realities of time and distance and travel mean that emigration to distant locales will limit one's ability to share time and resources with family, friends, and loved ones left behind. Emigration to a location within a few hours' drive, on the other hand, requires far fewer lifestyle changes.

Similarly, if emigration requires adaptation into a radically different culture and language, this will further limit the practicality of emigration for those who are not fluently multilingual. Thus, states have benefited considerably from the fact that many states enjoy monopolies on linguistic areas (which states reinforce through strategies like public education and the designation of "official" languages). For example, if one speaks only Swedish, one has a big incentive to stay in Sweden, and if one only speaks Greek, the personal cost of leaving Greece can be very high indeed. Even in the case of English, which is seen as being spoken internationally, it's significant that a majority of native English speakers live under a single state—the United States.[2] The implications of this for potential emigrants are evident.

---

[1] Kirkpatrick Sale, *Human Scale Revisited: A New Look at the Classic Case for a Decentralized Future* (White River Junction, Vt.: Chelsea Green Publishing, 2017), p. 145. In chapter 13, Sale discusses the proper size of the "optimum city." For Sale, most political jurisdictions are far too large, and Sale suggests a more reasonable size is between 50,000 and 100,000.

[2] Those who speak English as a second-language, or who speak a form of English creole are, of course, much more widespread and numerous than native speakers.

But, once states can extend their monopolies over vast expanses of land, linguistic areas, and cultural areas, emigration becomes even more difficult. States in these cases are more easily able to increase their taxation and regulatory power over a population without danger of losing significant amounts of tax revenue due to migration.

In the case of a small state, however, many of these cultural, linguistic, and distance-based barriers are greatly lessened. Were the United States actually composed of fifty (or more) truly independent political jurisdictions, residents could emigrate from region to region with less trouble in terms of adapting to local languages and culture. In the case of a move from Virginia to North Carolina, for example, it would still be practical in many cases for emigrants to regularly return to visit friends and family with relative ease.

This would become all the more true were these jurisdictions reduced in size even more—to the size of a metropolitan area or even a municipality.

In fact, we often see this at work even in partially decentralized political jurisdictions. In the US, for example, Americans and businesses often move across city and county lines to avoid certain regulations, to lower their taxes, or to take advantage of better amenities.

When the city of Chicago in 2006 imposed a number of high regulatory hurdles against Wal-Mart, the retail giant elected to simply move one block away from the Chicago city limit, thus depriving the city of tax revenues, but allowing Wal-Mart access to Chicago's consumer population.[3] If subunits in a confederation are appropriately small, "emigration" might be a matter of moving *a few miles* down the road, making the practical cost of emigration very low indeed.

---

[3]"Eighteen months after the Chicago City Council torpedoed a South Side Wal-Mart, 24,500 Chicagoans applied for 325 jobs at a Wal-Mart opening Friday in south suburban Evergreen Park, one block outside the city limits…. The new Wal-Mart at 2500 W. 95th is one block west of Western Avenue, the city boundary." Quoted in Craig DeLuz, "25,000 apply for 325 Walmart jobs….Project killed by Chicago City Council," *Craig DeLuz*, January 26, 2006, http://craigdeluz.com/25000-apply-for-325-walmart-jobs-project-killed-by-chicago-city-council/.

Life In a Microstate

Now, imagine a world composed of tiny states the size of small cities. The smaller the better. In our hypothetical world, let's imagine the city of Arcadia, California has become an independent republic. The city is eleven square miles with fifty-six thousand people. It borders at least five other cities. In other words, were the city an independent entity—we'll call it the Republic of Arcadia (ROA)—any resident need only move a few miles to change the government under which he or she lives.

Were the ROA to impose a large tax increase or a series of new onerous regulations, many residents would elect to move away. This situation would still impose costs on the new emigrants. They would perhaps need to sell their houses or businesses, which is costly in terms of time and money. By moving, they're leaving their preferred place of residence—which they had demonstrated by their previous actions was Arcadia. Now, however, they must live in a place that is their second or third choice, all else being equal.

In our Arcadia example, residents would have multiple choices of other jurisdictions with a nearly identical climate, language, and culture. Moreover, neighboring jurisdictions would likely be more than happy to accept the very people that the ROA's big tax hike is most likely to drive to emigrate: the most productive and entrepreneurial residents.

Monopoly vs. a "Marketplace" for States

In this scenario, the Republic of Arcadia is still formally a state in the strict sense. But even if the ROA has a state-like monopoly within its territory, this monopoly is limited to only that small piece of territory that falls within the ROA's jurisdiction. In other words, this "monopoly" is a very weak one indeed, and we are reminded that small states are less state-like than large states.

Of course, the presence of many choices doesn't mean everyone will always be able to find an ideal situation that meets all of his or her cultural, religious, and economic needs. Even in the world of mass-produced consumer goods, where competition is often fierce, a high degree of choice fails to provide *exactly* what each consumer imagines to be the ideal product.

Choices are always limited in real life, whether by physical geography, time, or by the willingness of others to voluntarily do business. One does not have the ability to choose a "perfect" hamburger restaurant at exactly the price point one desires, even in a vibrant and entrepreneurial marketplace. It is often impossible to find *exactly* the automobile one wants with the combination of features and with the appearance that perfectly matches each consumer's preferences. Unless one is wealthy enough to build a custom automobile from scratch, one can only pick from a number of available choices. In many cases the best we can do is simply to increase the number of options. The same holds true when it comes time to choose a regime under which to live.

Nonetheless, the presence of a high degree of competition and choice among separate regimes offers numerous opportunities to *improve* one's situation by relocating to a culturally similar, yet legally distinct political jurisdiction.

We Want More Borders and More States

One objection raised against a system of numerous independent states is the fact that some form of border control is likely to persist, and that multiple borders impose additional limitations on human rights—specifically the right to travel freely. Or, to use a term preferred by economists, we are told borders are bad because they impose "transaction costs" on the populations that wish to conduct business across these borders.

As we will see in later chapters, this concern is misplaced because in practice small states tend to be *more* open to the movement of goods, capital, and persons. Small states are less likely than large states to close themselves off from bordering regions. Nonetheless, some border controls are likely to persist even in this scenario. This is likely to impose at least a small cost on those who frequently wish to cross borders to visit family or access employment opportunities.

But a multitude of borders brings with it an often-ignored advantage in terms of protecting human rights and basic freedoms: borders also act as a *limit* on a state's powers. Put another way, just as borders impose transaction costs on the general population, they also tend to impose transaction costs on states themselves, limiting the abilities of states to exercise their own powers outside their own borders.

For example, East Germany's border with West Germany represented the limits of the East German police state, beyond which the power of the Stasi to kidnap, torture, and imprison peaceful people was far more limited than it was within its native jurisdiction. The West German border acted to contain the East German state.

Similarly, the borders of Saudi Arabia act as a limit to the Saudi regime's ability to impose its peculiar brand of brutal theocracy.

Even within a single nation-state, borders can illustrate the benefits of decentralization, as in the case of the Colorado-Nebraska border. On one side of the border (i.e., Nebraska) state police frequently arrest and imprison citizens for possessing marijuana. Those who resist will encounter the coercive violence of the state. On the other side of the border, the state's constitution prohibits police from prosecuting marijuana users. The Colorado border effectively places a limit on Nebraska's war on drugs.

Certainly, there are ways for regimes to extend their power even beyond their borders. This can be done by cozying up to the regimes of neighboring countries (or intimidating them), or through the organs of international quasi-state organizations. Or, as in the case of the United States and the European Union, imposing broader policies upon a number of supposedly sovereign states.

Nevertheless, thanks to the competitive nature of states, many states will often find it difficult to project their power into neighboring states, and thus borders represent a very-real impediment to a state's power. Yes, borders can offer impediments to free trade and free migration, but they also bring with them advantages in limiting the damage done by poorly run or despotic regimes. This can then open the door to greater freedom, and even save lives as certain states impoverish or make war on their own citizens. The existence of a border—especially for those who live near it—can offer greater access to resources beyond the reach of the regime under which one lives.

The Case of Venezuela

This principle was illustrated in recent years by the Venezuelan regime. For nearly twenty years, the Marxism-inspired regime has been expropriating and closing private businesses, while prosecuting entrepreneurs for trumped up "crimes" of exploiting the workers. Consequently, supply lines dried up and the nation entered into an economic crisis in which many goods and services became exceptionally scarce. By 2016, in order to avoid a serious humanitarian crisis, the regime opened its border with Colombia to allow Venezuelans the opportunity to purchase food and other supplies on the Colombian side of the border.[4]

Unlike the Venezuelan regime, the Colombian regime had not severely limited the capacity and freedoms of the private sector. Colombia had not reduced the country's population to desperate poverty amidst collapsing economic and social institutions.

Thus, at the time, it was rather easy to buy food and provisions on the Colombian side of the border while store shelves sat empty on the Venezuelan side.

In other words, the Colombian border acted both as a limit on the Venezuelan regime, and as a lifeline to Venezuela's residents; proximity to the border in this case was an *enhancement* of freedom rather than a limitation. Those who lived near the border were among the more fortunate residents of the country because the Colombian border became a source for essential goods and services either through legal trade, or through smuggling operations and illegal migration.

Borders As Protection from Supranational Superstates

Another advantage of borders—and the distinct territorial zones they create—is that they impose additional costs on supranational statelike organizations seeking to consolidate power and transform smaller states into mere components of large centralized states.

---

[4]Sibylla Brodzinsky, "Venezuelans storm Colombia border city in search of food and basic goods," *The Guardian*, July 5, 2016, https://www.theguardian.com/world/2016/jul/05/venezuelans-storm-colombia-border-food.

This can be seen most readily in the case of the European Union where the EU government in Brussels has sought to standardize, harmonize, and centralize power within the bloc. Yet, member states have continued to offer resistance to this centralizing impulse in many cases.

As described by Luigi Bassani and Carlo Lottieri:

> What is already happening in Europe is very significant. If present trends continue, the different European peoples…are about to be subject to the authority of a continental super-State. This new government will try to "harmonize" fiscal policies—not to lower taxes, to be sure—and every other type of control of individual resources. At the end perhaps, Brussels will command every political decision and succeed in building a new "imperial" State, alongside the United States.[5]

For now, however, proposed superstates such as the EU are "still unable to discipline States," meaning the power of the "continental super-state" is rendered far weaker because the budding international power is regarded as an "outside" force distinct from the persons and institutions within the borders of the resistant member states. The fact that each member state still, more or less, controls its own borders—and thus maintains a separate identity and jurisdiction—limits the power of the nascent EU state.

Bassani and Lottieri conclude there is a "certain irony" here. The smaller states—which are certainly states, and thus come with all the problems one would expect from states—are nonetheless obstacles to the creation of larger, even more abusive states.[6]

---

[5]Luigi Marco Bassani and Carlo Lottieri, "The Problem of Security: Historicity of the State and 'European Realism,'" in *The Myth of National Defense: Essays on the Theory and History of Security Production*, ed. Hans-Hermann Hoppe (Auburn, Ala.: Mises Institute, 2003), p. 61.

[6]Bassani and Lottieri write: "There is a certain irony in the fact that freedom seekers all around the globe must rely on the States' unwillingness to comply with the far-reaching political dreams of euro and world unificationists. The contemporary resistance of the State to this historical nemesis of its own logic—the same one that in the past has paved the road to the rise of political modernity and is now digging its grave—seems to be the only realistic hope

2

Political Anarchy
Is How the West Got Rich

I t is not uncommon to encounter political theorists and pundits who insist that political centralization is a boon to economic growth. In both cases, it is claimed the presence of a unifying central regime—whether in Brussels or in Washington, DC, for example—is essential in ensuring the efficient and free flow of goods throughout a large jurisdiction. This, we are told, will greatly accelerate economic growth.

In many ways, the model is the United States, inside of which there are virtually no barriers to trade or migration at all between member states. In the EU, barriers have been falling in recent decades.

The historical evidence, however, suggests that political unity is not actually a catalyst to economic growth or innovation over the long term. In fact, the European experience suggests that the opposite is true.

Why Did Europe Surpass China in Wealth and Growth?

A thousand years ago, a visitor from another planet might have easily overlooked Europe as a poor backwater. Instead, China and the Islamic world may have looked far more likely to be the world leaders in wealth and innovation indefinitely.

Why is it, then, that Europe became the wealthiest and most technologically advanced civilization in the world?

Indeed, the fact that Europe had grown to surpass other civilizations that were once more scientifically and technologically advanced had become apparent by the nineteenth century. Historians have debated the question of the origins of this "European miracle" ever since. This "miracle," historian Ralph Raico tells us:

> consists in a simple but momentous fact: It was in Europe—and the extensions of Europe, above all, America—that human beings first achieved per capita economic growth over a long period of time. In this way, European society eluded the "Malthusian trap," enabling new tens of millions to survive and the population as a whole to escape the hopeless misery that had been the lot of the great mass of the human race in earlier times. The question is: why Europe?[1]

Across the spectrum of historians, theories about Europe's economic development have been varied, to say the least.[2] But one of the most important characteristics of European civilization—ever since the collapse of the Western Roman Empire—has been Europe's political decentralization.

Raico continues:

> Although geographical factors played a role, the key to western development is to be found in the fact that, while Europe constituted a single civilization—Latin Christendom—it was at the same time radically decentralized. In contrast to other cultures—especially China, India, and the Islamic world—Europe

---

[1] Ralph Raico, "The Theory of Economic Development and the 'European Miracle'," in *The Collapse of Development Planning*, ed. Peter Boettke (New York: New York University Press, 1994), p. 39.

[2] Chiu Yu Ko, Mark Koyama, and Tuan-Hwee Sng, for example, contend China was forced to centralize due to threats from the Eurasian steppe. (See Chiu Yu Ko, Mark Koyama, Tuan-Hwee Sng, "Unified China and Divided Europe," *EH.net*, June 2014, http://eh.net/eha/wp-content/uploads/ 2014/05/Koyama. pdf.

comprised a system of divided and, hence, competing powers and jurisdictions.[3]

Although modern EU centralizers are attempting it, at no point has European civilization ever fallen under the dominion of a single state as has been the case in China. Even during the early modern period, as some polities managed to form absolutist states, much of Europe—such as the highly dynamic areas in the Low Countries, Northern Italy, and the German cities—remained in flux and highly decentralized. The rise of the merchant classes, banking, and an urban middle class—which began as early as the Middle Ages and were so essential in building industrial Europe—thrived without large states.

After all, while a large polity with few internal borders can indeed lead to large markets with fewer transaction costs, concentrating power in one place brings big risks; a state that can facilitate trade across a large empire is *also* a state that can stifle trade through regulation, taxation, and even expropriation.

The former vast kingdoms and empires of Asia may have once been well positioned to foster the creation of a wealthy merchant class and middle class. But the fact is this didn't happen. Those states instead focused on stifling threats to state power, centralizing political control of markets, and extorting the public through the imposition of fines and penalties on those who were disfavored by the ruling classes.

The Benefits of Anarchy

In contrast, Europe was relatively anarchic compared to other world civilizations and became the home of the great economic leap forward that we now take for granted. This isn't "anarchy" in the sense of "chaos," of course. This is anarchy as understood by political scientists: the lack of any single controlling state or authority. In key periods of the continent's development—as now—there was no

---

[3]Raico, "The Theory of Economic Development and the 'European Miracle'," p. 41.

ruler of "Europe" and no European empire. Thus, in his book *The Origins of Capitalism*, historian Jean Baechler concludes:

> The first condition for the maximization of economic efficiency is the liberation of civil society with respect to the state.... *The expansion of capitalism owes its origins and raison d'être to political anarchy.* (emphasis in original)[4]

For many years, economic historians have attempted to find correlations between this political anarchy and Europe's economic success. Many have found the connection to be undeniable. Economist Douglass North, for instance, writes:

> The failures of the most likely candidates, China and Islam, point the direction of our inquiry. Centralized political control limits the options—limits the alternatives that will be pursued in a context of uncertainty about the long-run consequences of political and economic decisions. It was precisely the lack of large scale political and economic order that created the environment essential to economic growth and ultimately human freedoms. In the competitive decentralized environment lots of alternatives were pursued; some worked, as in the Netherlands and England; some failed as

---

[4]Jean Baechler, *The Origins of Capitalism* (Oxford, U.K.: Basil Blackwell, 1975), pp. 77, 113. Baechler influenced F.A. Hayek in his thinking as well. Hayek quotes this passage in Baechler on "political anarchy" in volume 3 of *Law, Legislation and Liberty*. See F.A. Hayek, *Law, Legislation, and Liberty*, vol. 3 (Chicago: University of Chicago Press, 1979). Hayek also writes in *The Fatal Conceit*: "...the history of China provides many instances of government attempts to enforce so perfect an order that innovation became impossible. This country, technologically and scientifically developed so far ahead of Europe that, to give only one illustration, it had ten oil wells operating on one stretch of the river Po already in the twelfth century, certainly owed its later stagnation, but not its early progress, to the manipulatory power of its governments. What led the greatly advanced civilisation of China to fall behind Europe was its government's clamping down so tightly as to leave no room for new developments, while, as remarked in the last chapter, Europe probably owes its extraordinary expansion in the Middle Ages to its political anarchy." F.A. Hayek, *The Fatal Conceit: The Errors of Socialism*, ed. W.W. Barley, III (London: Routledge, 1988), p. 44.

in the case of Spain and Portugal; and some, such as France, fell in between these two extremes.[5]

Competition among Governments Means More Freedom

But why exactly does this sort of radical decentralization "limit the options" for ruling princes and kings? Freedom increases because under a decentralized system there are more "alternatives"—to use North's term—available to those seeking to avoid what E.L. Jones calls "predatory government tax behavior." Thus, historian David Landes emphasized the importance of "multiple, competing polities" in Europe in setting the stage for:

> private enterprise in the West possess[ing] a social and political vitality without precedent or counterpart. This varied, needless to say, from one part of Europe to another....And sometimes adventitious events like war or a change of sovereign produced a major alteration in the circumstances of the business classes. On balance, however, the place of private enterprise was secure and improving with time; and this is apparent in the institutional arrangements that governed the getting and spending of wealth.[6]

It was this "latent competition between states," Jones contends, that drove individual polities to pursue policies designed to attract capital.[7] More competent princes and kings adopted policies that led to economic prosperity in neighboring polities, and thus "freedom of movement among the nation-states offered opportunities for 'best practices' to diffuse in many spheres, not least the economic." Since European states were relatively small and weak—yet culturally similar to many neighboring jurisdictions—abuses of power by the ruling classes led to declines in both revenue and in the

---

[5]Douglass North, "The Paradox of the West," in *The Origins of Modern Freedom in the West*, ed. R.W. Davis (Stanford, Calif.: Stanford University Press, 1995).

[6]David Landes, *The Unbound Prometheus: Technological Change and Industrial Development in Western Europe from 1750 to the Present* (Cambridge, U.K.: Cambridge University Press, 1969), p. 15.

[7]E.L. Jones, *The European Miracle: Environments, Economies and Geopolitics in the History of Europe and Asia* (Cambridge, U.K.: Cambridge University Press, 2003), p. 118.

most valuable residents. Rulers sought to counter this by guaranteeing protections for private property.

This doesn't mean there were never abuses of power, of course,
but as Landes observed:

> To be sure, kings could, and did, make or break men of business;
> but the power of the sovereign was constrained by the require-
> ments of states…and international competition. Capitalists could
> take their wealth and enterprise elsewhere and even if they could
> not leave, the capitalists of other realms would not be slow to profit
> from their discomfiture.[8]

Nor was decentralization limited to the international system
of separate sovereign states. Thanks to the longtime tug-of-war
between the state and the church, and between kings and nobles,
decentralization was common even *within* polities. Raico continues:

> Decentralization of power also came to mark the domestic
> arrangements of the various European polities. Here feudalism—
> which produced a nobility rooted in feudal right rather than in
> state-service—is thought by a number of scholars to have played
> an essential role….Through the struggle for power within the
> realms, representative bodies came into being, and princes often
> found their hands tied by the charters of rights (Magna Carta, for
> instance) which they were forced to grant their subjects. In the
> end, even within the relatively small states of Europe, power was
> dispersed among estates, orders, chartered towns, religious com-
> munities, corps, universities, etc., each with its own guaranteed
> liberties.[9]

---

[8]Landes, *The Unbound Prometheus*, p. 15.

[9]Raico, p. 42. It is important to note Raico does not treat Latin Christendom's
"radical decentralization" as something that "just happened." That is, I think Andrei Znamenski is reading Raico incorrectly when Znamenski states the framework which stresses the "role of political fragmentation and decentralization as
the major factor that allowed Europe to spread its economic wings" is "a well-
taken and well-supported one," but concludes "it leaves unanswered the simple
question of how the fragmentation and decentralization came into existence
in the first place." Raico does address this by noting it was specifically *Western* Europe, which was the most economically successful and non-coincidentally
existed under the Latin Church's opposition to any single civil government

Over the long term, however, it was the system of international anarchy that appears to have ensured that states were constrained in their ability to tax and extort the merchant classes and middle classes, who were such a key component of Europe's rising economic fortunes.[10]

We Need a Return to Smaller Polities

Even today, we continue to see these factors at work. Small states—especially in Europe and the Americas—tend to have higher incomes and have greater openness. We can see this in the microstates of Europe and in the Caribbean. Small states, seeking to attract capital, often undercut larger neighbors in terms of taxes.

It is true that one of the most economically successful polities in the world today is a large one: the United States. The US's success, however, can be attributed to the enduring presence of political decentralization internally—especially during the nineteenth century—and to the latent, albeit receding, economic liberalism esteemed by much of its population. Europe, of course, was already rich—and relatively politically free compared to the despotic regimes of the East—long before it began to centralize political power under the banner of the European Union.

---

becoming the ultimate civil power in Europe. See Andrei Znamenski, "The 'European Miracle' Warrior Aristocrats, Spirit of Liberty, and Competitionas a Discovery Process," *The Independent Review* 16, no. 4 (Spring 2012).

[10] The importance of decentralization within states cannot be ignored, of course. As historian Joel Mokyr notes in "The Enduring Riddle of the European Miracle: The Enlightenment and the Industrial Revolution" (2002), the rise of political and economic liberalism (which he calls "the Enlightenment") was key in weakening states in their ability to enrich entrenched rent seeking interests at the expense of market producers. This, however, does not undermine our theory of decentralization since decentralization is a key component in sustaining and laying the groundwork necessary for ideological liberalism to thrive. See Joel Mokyr, "The Enduring Riddle of the European Miracle: The Enlightenment and the Industrial Revolution," October 2002, http://citeseerx.ist.psu.edu/viewdoc/download?doi=10.1.1.477.6576&rep=rep1&type=pdf.

Today, however, we are seeing the impoverishing downside of decades of political centralization in both the US and Europe. Government regulations decreed from Brussels and Washington continue to stifle innovation and entrepreneurship. The EU has sought to crack down on low taxes in smaller member states. Both the EU and the US are erecting trade barriers to producers outside their trading blocs.

Unfortunately, those in power, who benefit from the status quo and from holding the reins of large states, are unlikely to relinquish this newly gained power without a fight.

3

Why Regimes Prefer Big States and Centralized Power

W hen the Soviet Union began its collapse in 1989, the world witnessed decentralization and secession on a broad scale.

Over the next several years, puppet regimes and states that were independent in name only broke away from Soviet domination and formed sovereign states. Some states which had completely ceased to exist—such as the Baltic states—declared independence and became states in their own right. In its heyday, the Soviet Union had been three times the size of the United States, and was controlled by a regime with nearly untrammeled power consolidated in a centralized state. In its place rose a number of new regimes that were smaller in size and smaller in population.

In total, secession and decentralization in this era brought about more than a dozen newly independent states.[1]

---

[1] This was part of an even larger global trend from 1950 to 2000. During this period, the total number of independent nations almost doubled to 191. Many of these new states were formed out of Europe-based empires that slowly collapsed during the 1950s and 1960s.

Political decisions that had once been made unilaterally in Moscow now were being made in numerous places; places like Riga in Lithuania, Kiev in Ukraine, and Yerevan in Armenia. This period served as an important reminder that human history is not, in fact, just a story of ever-increasing state power and centralization.

Since then, however, the world has seen few successful secession movements. A handful of new countries have come into being over the past twenty years, such as East Timor and South Sudan. But in spite of many efforts by separatists worldwide, there have been few changes to the lines on the maps.

This has certainly been the case in Europe and the Americas, where from Quebec to Scotland to Catalonia to Venice demands for independence have been met with trepidation and sometimes outright threats of violence from central governments.[2]

Benefits of Bigness:
More Sources of Wealth for Costly State Institutions

State opposition to any movement toward dismemberment is partly due to the fact that state organizations—that is, the people who control them—are motivated to cling to the benefits conferred by bigness.

Much of this stems from the nature of states themselves. The ideology underpinning the modern sovereign state—also known as the "Westphalian state"—is founded largely on the idea that states ought to secure and protect a monopoly on the means of coercion within a specific territory. This process of statebuilding often involved the physical invasion of independent regions and territories within a potential state's territory, and the neutralization of any military forces answerable to local nobles or municipal governments. As a state's rulers sought to consolidate power, they pursued new ways to

---

[2]Nick Squires, "Venice prepares for referendum on secession from Italy," *The Telegraph*. March 14, 2014, https://www.telegraph.co.uk/news/worldnews/europe/italy/10698299/Venice-prepares-for-referendum-on-secession-from-Italy.html.

limit the power of local power centers such as cities, guilds, religious organizations and the local nobility. When successful, this strategy enabled state rulers to control resources directly rather than indirectly through local institutions. Ideally, state rulers built up large state bureaucracies answerable to—and funded directly by—the central state. More specifically, states must, as described by political scientist Charles Tilly,

> Produce distinct organizations that control the chief concentrated means of coercion within well-defined territories, and exercise priority in some respects over all other organizations operating within those territories. Efforts to subordinate neighbors and fight off more distant rivals create state structures in the form not only of armies but also of civilian staff that gather the means to sustain armies and that organize the ruler's day-to-day control over the rest of the civilian population.[3]

According to Tilly, these "distinct organizations" clearly include armies, but they also include organizations such as police, a bureaucracy for collecting taxes, and a prison system. Most important are the institutions that ensure physical control over the state's potential enemies both foreign and domestic. As Murray Rothbard has noted:

> What the State fears above all, of course, is any fundamental threat to its own power and its own existence. The death of a State can come about in two major ways: (a) through conquest by another State, or (b) through revolutionary overthrow by its own subjects—in short, by war or revolution. War and revolution, as the two basic threats, invariably arouse in the State rulers their maximum efforts and maximum propaganda among the people.[4]

The occasional need for "maximum propaganda" also highlights a state's need for "soft power." This generally includes educational institutions and other organizations that employ intellectuals to help convince the population that a state is both beneficial and necessary.

---

[3]Charles Tilly, *Coercion, Capital, and European States: AD 990–1992* (Malden, Mass.: Blackwell Publishers, 1992), p. 19.

[4]Murray N. Rothbard, "Anatomy of the State," mises.org, 2009, https://mises.org/library/anatomy-state.

The supposed benefits of state power to the general public can also be displayed through a welfare state. This aspect of extending state power did not develop much sophistication until the nineteenth century when the German Otto von Bismarck "established compulsory accident, sickness, and old-age insurance for workers."[5] That is, he took the first steps toward a permanent and bureaucratic "safety net" for the population within Bismarck's newly crafted German empire. But, as Robert Higgs recognized, "Bismarck was no altruist. He intended his social programs to divert workingmen from revolutionary socialism and to purchase their loyalty to the Kaiser's regime; to a large extent he seems to have achieved his objectives."[6]

Welfare states need not be established out of cynical motives, of course, but their end effect is the same. As Martin van Creveld observes, the welfare state was essential in "tightening the state's grip on the economy" which had the additional benefit of "eradicating or at least greatly weakening lesser institutions" which had provided charity and economic benefits in earlier times.[7]

Naturally, this is all very costly to the state, so states will tend to seek direct access to reliable sources of wealth and geopolitical power. This can often be augmented through growth in either physical size or population—or both.

By this way of thinking, the most safe and secure states are those that can best physically control the means of military defense, punish the disobedient, dole out economic benefits, and provide funding to teachers and intellectuals.

For example, greater size means a larger frontier that can act as a physical buffer between the state's enemies and the state's economic core. Physical size is also helpful in terms of pursuing self-sufficiency in both energy production and agriculture. More land means greater

---

[5]Robert Higgs, "The Welfare State and the Promise of Protection," *Mises Daily*, August 24, 2009, https://mises.org/library/welfare-state-and-promise-protection.

[6]Ibid.

[7]Martin Van Creveld, *The Rise and Decline of the State* (Cambridge, U.K.: Cambridge University Press, 1999), pp. 354–56.

potential for resource extraction and acreage devoted to food production. The wages and capital accumulation that arises from these activities can also be taxed, expropriated, or otherwise controlled to benefit the state itself.

In terms of population size, state control over larger populations means more human workers to tax. Larger populations also provide personnel for military uses.

Naturally, state organizations are not inclined to abandon these advantages lightly, even if a sizable portion of the population begins to move in the direction of secession.

Why States Sometimes Get Smaller

Sometimes, though, states are forced to contract in size and scope. This usually happens when the cost of maintaining the status quo becomes higher than the cost of allowing a region to gain autonomy.

Historically, the cost to the state of maintaining unity is raised through military means. Once a region in rebellion becomes sufficiently costly, it is abandoned by the outgoing central government.[8] Examples of this tactic being successfully employed include the cases of the United States, the Republic of Ireland, and some of the successor states of Yugoslavia.[9]

But secession and decentralization have also often been achieved through bloodless or near bloodless means. This was the case in Iceland in 1944 and throughout most of the post-Iron Curtain states.

Bloodless secession movements, however, tend to enjoy the most success when the parent state is weakened by larger events beyond the secession movement itself. Iceland, for example, seceded in 1944 when World War II ensured that Denmark was in no position to

---

[8]Jörg Guido Hülsmann, "Secession and the Production of Defense," in *The Myth of National Defense*, ed. Hans-Hermann Hoppe (Auburn, Ala.: Mises Institute, 2003), p. 380.

[9]The Republic of Ireland employed violence to obtain independence, although it is unlikely that Ireland would have obtained independence when it did had the British state not been weakened by the First World War.

object.[10] The post-Soviet states seceded when the Soviet state had been rendered impotent by decades of economic decline and (in 1991) a failed coup.[11] Nor is it a coincidence that India gained independence from the United Kingdom in the years immediately following World War II. It is likely the UK could have held on to India through military means indefinitely, but this would have come at a very high cost to the British economy and standard of living.

It is possible to envision largely "amicable" separations. The model for this is the separation of Canada, Australia, and New Zealand from the United Kingdom. But even in these cases, British control over these Commonwealth states' foreign policy was not totally abandoned until after World War II, when the British state had been weakened by depression and war. Moreover, the British state assumed that these newly independent states would remain highly reliable geopolitical and economic allies indefinitely. Thus, the geopolitical cost of separation was perceived to be low.

Mega-States Are the Ideal State
(From the State's Perspective)

In cases where the seceding state is perceived to have different cultural, economic, or geopolitical interests—which is true of the overwhelming majority of cases—the parent state is, all else being equal, likely to meet demands for secession with much hostility.

Although liberal ideology has diminished the perception among much of the world's population that bigger is better, most government agents—who are by nature decidedly illiberal—see things differently. For them, the ideal state is most certainly a large state.

---

[10]In a 1918 plebiscite, Iceland's voters approved independence for the country in a personal union with Denmark under the Danish king. (The king would remain the head of state. Iceland became a republic after another plebiscite in 1944.)

[11]Specifically, the "August Coup" of 1991 during which Soviet hardliners attempted to seize control of the regime from Mikhail Gorbachev.

Those who delight in the generous application of state violence have noticed that it is not a coincidence that the world's most powerful states—e.g., the US, Russia, China—are often those that control large populations, large economic centers, and large geographic areas with sizable frontiers. The combination of these three factors in various configurations ensures that existential threats to the regime are few and far between. Russia's relatively small economy—only a fraction of the size of Germany's economy—is mitigated by its enormous geographical frontiers. Its economy is nonetheless large *enough* to maintain a nuclear arsenal. China's *per capita* wealth is quite small, but Chinese territory, its limited nuclear arsenal, and the sheer size of its overall economy ensure a high degree of protection from foreign attack. The US's enormous economy and its huge ocean frontiers render it essentially immune to all existential threats other than large-scale nuclear war.

Large states such as these are limited only by the military capabilities of other states, and by the threat of domestic unrest and resistance.

Totalitarian States Require Bigness

This relationship between bigness and state power has been illustrated in the fact that totalitarian states are virtually always large states.

In her book *The Origins of Totalitarianism*, Hannah Arendt examines a number of nontotalitarian dictatorships that sprang up in Europe before the Second World War. These included (among others) the Baltic states, Hungary, Portugal, and Romania. In many of these cases, Arendt contends the regimes *attempted* to turn themselves into totalitarian regimes, but failed. This was largely due to their lack of size:

> Although [totalitarian ideology] had served well enough to organize the masses until the movement seized power, the absolute size of the country then forced the would-be totalitarian ruler of masses into the more familiar patterns of class or party dictatorship. The truth is that these countries simply did not control enough human material to allow for total domination and its inherent great losses in population. Without much hope for the

conquest of more heavily populated territories, the tyrants in these small countries were forced into a certain old-fashioned moderation lest they lose whatever people they had to rule. This is also why Nazism, up to the outbreak of the war and its expansion over Europe, lagged so far behind its Russian counterpart in consistency and ruthlessness; even the German people were not numerous enough to allow for the full development of this newest form of government. Only if Germany had won the war would she have known a fully developed totalitarian rulership.[12]

Arendt was not an economist, but had she been one, she might have noted that the necessity of size is so central to totalitarian regimes because they are so economically inefficient. Contrary to promises of machine-like efficiency made by advocates of ever more powerful states, totalitarian states are absurdly wasteful both in terms of capital and human life. The same is true—to varying extents—for *all* regimes. But as the most centrally-planned ones—whether totalitarian or not—quickly become economic basket cases, large size is necessary.[13] A smaller state would quickly exhaust its capital and its population, and the regime would collapse. Size can provide the appearance of sustainability for longer.

Cultural factors cannot be ignored, however. Arendt concedes this process of collapse can be drawn out longer in societies that are more ideologically tolerant of it:

> Conversely, the chances for totalitarian rule are frighteningly good in the lands of traditional Oriental despotism, in India and China...[14]

That region's relative tolerance for despotism is enabled by local ideologies that foster a "feeling of superfluousness," which according

---

[12]Hannah Arendt, *The Origins of Totalitarianism* (New York: Harcourt, 1976), p. 310.

[13]Centrally-planned economies fall victim to what Ludwig von Mises called the economic calculation problem, and quickly become wasteful and inefficient in proportion to the degree to which the private-sector economy is socialized. See Ludwig von Mises, "Economic Calculation in the Socialist Commonwealth" (Auburn, Ala.: Mises Institute, 2012).

[14]Arendt, *The Origins of Totalitarianism*, p. 311.

to Arendt "has been prevalent for centuries in the contempt for the value of human life."[15]

None of this means the world is now absent of small states that attempt to maximize the regime's power. Some small states, such as North Korea, have maintained an economically isolationist and totalitarian stance—fueled both by internal paranoia and by real perennial threats issued by the regime's enemies. For the most part, however, the spread of markets (and promarket ideology) has raised the opportunity cost of militaristic expansion from the state's perspective. If offered the chance to expand at low cost, though, virtually all regimes would take the opportunity in a heartbeat. And this is why we will likely continue to see regimes enthusiastically resist secession within their own borders. States don't have many opportunities to expand their territories and populations. So they're not about to sign off on secession lightly. Nevertheless, new economic realities, wars, and demographic shifts may certainly affect the equation in coming years. And then we may again see a redrawing of maps of a sort not seen since the end of the Cold War.

---

[15]Ibid.

4

Why the Classical Liberals Wanted Decentralization

n recent decades, many pundits, scholars, and intellectuals have assured us that advances in communications and transportation would eliminate the different political, economic, and cultural characteristics peculiar to residents of different regions within the United States. It is true that the cultural difference between a rural mechanic and an urban barista is smaller today than was the case in 1900. Yet recent national elections suggest that geography is still an important factor in understanding the many differences that prevail across regions within the US. Urban centers, suburban neighborhoods, and rural towns are still characterized by certain cultural, religious, and economic interests that are hardly uniform nationwide.

In a country as large as the United States, of course, this has long been a reality of American life. But even in smaller countries, such as the larger states of Europe, the problem of creating a national regime designed to rule over a large diverse population has long preoccupied political theorists. At the same time, the problem of *limiting* this state power has especially been of interest to proponents of liberalism—including its modern variant, "libertarianism"—who are concerned with protecting property rights and other human rights from abuses inflicted by political regimes.

The Growth of the State
and the Decline of Local Powers

Among the best observers and critics of the problem of state power were the great French liberals of the nineteenth century, who watched this process of centralization unfold during the rise of absolutism under the Bourbon monarchy and during the revolution.[1]

Many of these liberals understood how historical local autonomy in cities and regions throughout France had offered resistance to these efforts to centralize and consolidate the French state's power.[2]

Alexis de Tocqueville explains the historical context in *Democracy in America*:

> During the aristocratic ages which preceded the present time, the sovereigns of Europe had been deprived of, or had relinquished, many of the rights inherent in their power. Not a hundred years

---

[1]Murray Rothbard also viewed the rise of French absolutism as an attack on local control and local prerogatives. See Ryan McMaken, "Medievalism, Absolutism, and the French Revolution," *Mises Wire*, July 12, 2019.

[2]It is important to note that many liberals also supported the centralization of power. On this, Jörg Guido Hülsmann writes:

> To get rid of aristocratic privileges, the classical liberals first supported the king against the lesser aristocrats, and then concentrated further powers in the democratic central state to fight all regional and local forms of monarchism and aristocracy. Rather than curbing political power, they merely shifted and centralized it, creating even more powerful political institutions than those they were trying to supersede. The classical liberals thus bought their short-run successes with very burdensome long-run annuities, some of which we have paid in the twentieth century....It is true that this "technique" was very effective in realizing the classical-liberal program all at once in the whole territory controlled by the new democratic central state. Without it, this process would have been gradual, and it would have implied that islands of the *Ancien Régime* would have survived for a very long time. Yet like all mere techniques, this was a two-edged sword that would eventually be turned against life, liberty, and property.

See Jörg Guido Hülsmann, "Secession and the Production of Defense," in *The Myth of National Defense*, ed. Hans-Hermann Hoppe (Auburn, Ala.: Mises Institute, 2003), p. 380.

ago, amongst the greater part of European nations, numerous private persons and corporations were sufficiently independent to administer justice, to raise and maintain troops, to levy taxes, and frequently even to make or interpret the law.[3]

These "secondary powers" provided numerous centers of political power beyond the reach and control of the centralized powers held by the French state.[4] But by the late eighteenth century, they were rapidly disappearing:

> At the same period a great number of secondary powers existed in Europe, which represented local interests and administered local affairs. Most of these local authorities have already disappeared; all are speedily tending to disappear, or to fall into the most complete dependence. From one end of Europe to the other the privileges of the nobility, the liberties of cities, and the powers of provincial bodies, are either destroyed or upon the verge of destruction.[5]

This, Tocqueville understood, was no mere accident and did not occur without the approval and encouragement of national sovereigns. Although these trends were accelerated in France by the revolution, this was not limited to France, and there were larger ideological and sociological trends at work:

> The State has everywhere resumed to itself alone these natural attributes of sovereign power; in all matters of government the State tolerates no intermediate agent between itself and the people,

---

[3]Alexis de Tocqueville, *Democracy in America*, vol. 2, bk. 4, chap. 5, https://en.wikisource.org/wiki/Democracy_in_America/Volume_2/Book_4/Chapter_5.

[4]An important characteristic of the pre-absolutist and pre-modern political institutions was that they often failed to achieve monopoly power within their jurisdictions. That is, power was often shared between the national sovereign and by local authorities, and government relied much more on a consensus model rather than on government-by-decree from a central authority. See Luigi Marco Bassani and Carlo Lottieri, "The Problem of Security: Historicity of the State and 'European Realism'," in *The Myth of National Defense*, ed. Hans-Hermann Hoppe (Auburn, Ala.: Mises Institute 2003), p. 35.

[5]Tocqueville, *Democracy in America*.

and in general business it directs the people by its own immediate influence.[6]

Naturally, powerful states are not enthusiastic about having to work through intermediaries when the central state could instead exercise *direct* power through its bureaucracy and by employing a centrally controlled machinery of coercion. Thus, if states can dispense with the inconveniences of "local sovereignty" this enables the sovereign power to exercise its own power all the more completely.

The Power of Local Allegiance and Local Customs

When states are dominated by any single political center, other centers of social and economic life often arise in opposition. This is because human society is by nature quite diverse in itself, and especially so across different regions and cities. Different economic realities, different religions, and different demographics (among other factors) tend to produce a wide range of diverse views and interests. Over time, these habits and interests supported in a particular time and place begin to form into local "traditions" of various sorts.

Benjamin Constant came to similar conclusions. As noted by historian Ralph Raico: "Constant appreciated the importance of voluntary traditions, those generated by the free activity of society itself....Constant emphasized the value of these old ways in the struggle against state power."[7]

In his book *Principles of Politics Applicable to All Governments*, Constant complains that many liberals of his time, having been influenced by Montesquieu, embraced the ideal of uniformity in laws and political institutions.

This, Constant warns, is a mistake and tends to create more powerful centralized states, which then proceed to violate the very rights that Montesquieu thought could be preserved through uniformity.

---

[6]Ibid.

[7]Ralph Raico, *Classical Liberalism and the Austrian School* (Auburn, Ala.: Mises Institute, 2012), p. 225.

But political uniformity can lead down very dangerous paths, Constant insists, concluding, "It is by sacrificing everything to exaggerated ideas of uniformity that large States have become a scourge for humanity."[8] This is because large politically uniform states can only reach this level of uniformity by employing the state's coercive power to force uniformity on the people. The people do not give up their local traditions and institutions easily and therefore, Constant continues,

> It is clear that different portions of the same people, placed in circumstances, brought up in customs, living in places, which are all dissimilar, cannot be led to absolutely the same manners, usages, practices, and laws, without a coercion which would cost them more than it is worth.[9]

This may not be "worth it" to the people, but it appears to be worth it to the regime. Thus, states over the past several centuries have expended immense amounts of time and treasure to break down local resistance, impose national languages, and homogenize national institutions. When this process is successful, a nation's laws end up reflecting the preferences and concerns of those from the dominant region or population at the expense of everyone else. When it comes to these large centralized states, Constant writes:

> one must not underestimate their multiple and terrible drawbacks. Their size requires an activism and force at the heart of government which is difficult to contain and degenerates into despotism. The laws come from a point so far from those to whom they are supposed to apply that the inevitable effect of such distance is serious and frequent error. Local injustices never reach the heart of government. Placed in the capital, it takes the views of its surrounding area or at the very most of its place of residence for those of the whole State. A local or passing circumstance thus becomes the reason for a general law, and the inhabitants of the most distant provinces are

---

[8]Benjamin Constant, *Principles of Politics Applicable to All Governments*, tr., Dennis O'Keeffe, ed. Etienne Hofmann (Indianapolis, Ind.: Liberty Fund, 2003), https://oll.libertyfund.org/title/constant-principles-of-politics-applicable-to-all-governments.

[9]Ibid.

suddenly surprised by unexpected innovations, unmerited severity, vexatious regulations, undermining the basis of all their calculations, and all the safeguards of their interests, because two hundred leagues away men who are total strangers to them had some inkling of agitation, divined certain needs, or perceived certain dangers.[10]

For Constant, the diversity among communities ought not to be seen as a problem to be solved, but rather as a bulwark against state power. Moreover, it is not enough to speak only of *individual* freedoms and prerogatives when discussing the limits of state power. Rather, it is important to actively encourage local institutional independence as well:

Local interests and memories contain a principle of resistance which government allows only with regret and which it is keen to uproot. It makes even shorter work of individuals. It rolls its immense mass effortlessly over them, as over sand.[11]

Ultimately, this local institutional strength is key because, for Constant, state power can be successfully limited when it is possible to "skillfully combine institutions and place within them certain counterweights against the vices and weaknesses of men."[12]

The sentiments of Tocqueville and Constant were echoed later in the nineteenth century by Gustave de Molinari who came to similar conclusions:

In many respects the ancient customs, adapted over centuries to the populations they ruled and successively perfected by way of experiment, left a much greater area to individual liberty and established the responsibility attaching to liberty with more equity.[13]

---

[10]Ibid.

[11]Ibid.

[12]Ralph Raico, "Great Individualists of the Past: Benjamin Constant," *New Individualist Review* (Indianapolis, Ind.: Liberty Fund, 1981), https://oll.libertyfund.org/page/raico-on-benjamin-constant.

[13]Quoted in Raico, *Classical Liberalism and the Austrian School*, p. 242.

Molinari would take these historical observations, however, and come to even more radical conclusions than most French liberals. In an essay titled "The Production of Security," Molinari denounced the very idea of "monopoly government," concluding that competition among regimes was beneficial even within a single territory. When monopoly power prevails, Molinary writes, "justice becomes costly and slow, the police vexatious, individual liberty ceases to be respected, and the price of security is abusively high and unequally levied."[14]

The American Example: An Independent State

Nonetheless, Molinari's more radical views were a minority position. As we see in the work of Constant and Tocqueville, the French liberals were often advocating for decentralization within a larger political entity. In this way of thinking the French state—and other states—were a given, albeit something that could be improved by significantly decentralizing the state's power.

By the time French liberalism became a meaningful political force, however, the American liberals had already provided their own example of decentralization, in a form far more radical: the secession of the American colonies from the British Empire.

In contrast to the French liberal example of internal decentralization, the American example was of total separation. The end game in this case was to establish a completely independent state—or *group* of independent states.

The underlying philosophy behind this is clear enough in the text of the American colonials' Declaration of Independence—penned primarily by Thomas Jefferson. The argument is simple: universal human rights are important, and political regimes are only legitimate or valuable when they can be relied upon to protect those rights. If a regime violates these rights, then it may be necessary to break off from that regime and form an independent state.

---

[14]Ibid., p. 239

Yet even as the Americans moved increasingly toward forming a single confederation in North America, they were careful to ensure this was a *decentralized* state with political power spread out among a number of smaller member states. As originally conceived, the central government was to be quite weak. There was to be no standing federal army, and most land-based military power was to be in the hands of the militias controlled by member states. Local legislatures and local courts were to handle the overwhelming majority of government administration. Federal powers were to be strictly limited in comparison to more flexible powers of member states.

Especially among the more decentralization-minded American revolutionaries—such as Jefferson and the many "Anti-Federalists," who opposed ratification of the new constitution without a Bill of Rights—it was thought that local customs and local institutions could provide a barrier against the abuse of power by the new national government.[15]

This ideology would continue to be a political force for another century under the Jeffersonians and Jacksonians who were perennially suspicious of federal power.[16]

Liberal Decentralization in Decline

Today, however, liberal efforts to protect regional power and customs from encroachment by central governments are very much in decline. Whether it is attacks on Brexit in Europe, or denunciations of so-called "states' rights" in the United States, even limited and weak appeals to local control and self-determination are met with

---

[15]Prior to the Fourteenth Amendment, the Bill of Rights limited federal power only, and explicitly reserved the exercise of most powers and prerogatives to the member states or "the people" as stated in the Tenth Amendment.

[16]Rothbard regarded the Democratic Party in the nineteenth century, which was largely controlled by Jacksonians, to be a true laissez-faire liberal political party. This ended in 1896 when William Jennings Bryan fundamentally changed the ideological orientation of the party away from laissez-faire. Murray N. Rothbard, "1896: The Collapse of the Third Party System and of Laissez-faire Politics," *The Progressive Era*, ed. Patrick Newman (Auburn, Ala.: Mises Institute, 2017), p. 163.

contempt from countless pundits, politicians, and intellectuals. Two centuries after Tocqueville and Constant, regimes still see decentralization as a threat. And they are right. Decentralization *is* a threat to state power. Those who seek to limit political power in the liberal tradition ought to take notice.

5

Secession as a Path to Self-Determination

One of the most consistent and enthusiastic defenders of human rights and "natural rights" in the twentieth century was the economist and historian Murray Rothbard. A self-described libertarian, Rothbard would also have fit in well among the more radical liberals of the nineteenth century such as the Belgian-French economist Gustave de Molinari and the American anarchist Lysander Spooner.

Like Spooner—a New England abolitionist who advocated for the dissolution of the United States through secession—Rothbard supported the "radical decentralization" of the state. Indeed, Rothbard regarded secession and other forms of decentralization as central to limiting the power of sovereign states—which he regarded as critical in lessening the abuses inflicted by regimes on the population.

For example, in May 1969, Rothbard published an editorial in *Libertarian Forum* endorsing the mayoral candidacy of Norman Mailer. Specifically, Rothbard backed Mailer's support for the idea of decentralizing New York's gargantuan city government into a number of much smaller neighborhood governments. Rothbard also presumably liked Mailer's idea "that New York City secede from

New York State and form a separate 51st State." Decentralizing New York's government, Rothbard concluded, was:

> a position not only consistent with breaking up large governmental bodies but also with the crucial libertarian principle of secession. Secession is a crucial part of the libertarian philosophy: that every state be allowed to secede from the nation, every sub-state from the state, every neighborhood from the city, and, logically, every individual or group from the neighborhood.[1]

Later, in a 1977 editorial supporting the secession of Quebec from Canada, Rothbard wrote:

> There are two positive reasons for the libertarian to cheer at the imminent achievement of Quebec Independence. In the first place, secession—the breaking up of a State from within—is a great good in itself for any libertarian. It means that a giant central State is being broken up into constituent parts; it means greater competition between governments of different geographical areas, enabling people of one State to zip across the border to relatively greater freedom more easily; and it exalts the mighty libertarian principle of secession, which we hope to extend on down from the region to the city to the block to the individual.[2]

We find in the pages of *Libertarian Forum* numerous calls for secession around the globe. Rothbard penned editorials supporting the secession of Biafra from Nigeria. He lamented the US's intervention in the "secession movement" of Moise Tschombe in what is now the Democratic Republic of the Congo, and which led to "an artificially centralized Congo."[3]

In 1983, Rothbard supported the separation of Greek Cyprus from Turkish Cyprus, denouncing the US state's call for unity. Roth-

---

[1]Murray N. Rothbard, "Mailer for Mayor," *The Libertarian Forum*, May 15, 1969, p. 17.

[2]Murray N. Rothbard, "Vive Le Quebec Libre," *The Libertarian Forum*, January 1977, p. 8.

[3]Murray N. Rothbard, "US Out of Angola!," *The Libertarian Forum*, January 1976, p. 1.

bard asked, "why *shouldn't* the Turkish minority on Cyprus have the power to secede and set up their own republic?" (, in original).[4]

This is all in line with passages from Rothbard's book *Power and Market*. In the chapter on "Defenses on the Free Market," Rothbard noted that almost no one insists that in order to function, human society requires one single state to impose a just system of law. In fact, many recognize that the establishment of a single global mega-state comes with many downsides. So, given that it is acceptable that there be more than one political entity, the principle ought to be merely expanded down to the most basic level possible:

> If Canada and the United States can be separate nations without being denounced as being in a state of impermissible "anarchy," why may not the South secede from the United States? New York State from the Union? New York City from the state? Why may not Manhattan secede? Each neighborhood? Each block? Each house? Each *person*?[5]

Needless to say, Rothbard comes down on the prosecession side of this debate.

During the 1990s, Rothbard supported numerous cases of secession during the breakup of the old Iron Curtain, including in the Baltic states, Slovenia, and Czechoslovakia. In 1994, he continued to push for the breaking up of the old Soviet Union and all other large states—including the United States—contending:

> In short, every group, every nationality, should be allowed to secede from any nation-state and to join any other nation-state that agrees to have it.[6]

But if Rothbard regarded individual freedom as the most important *political* value—not to be confused with the most important value *overall*—why did he regard secession as so important? After

---

[4]Murray N. Rothbard, "Reagan War Watch," *The Libertarian Forum*, November-December, 1983, p. 8.
[5]Murray N. Rothbard, "Nations by Consent," *The Journal of Libertarian Studies* 11, no. 1 (Fall 1994), https://mises.org/library/nations-consent.
[6]Ibid.

all, secession in itself does not *guarantee* more freedom to the inhabitants of the new, smaller jurisdiction.

Rothbard pushed secession for two main reasons: First, he regarded it as a useful tactic in *moving toward his ideal* of maximum individual freedom. Second, even when this ideal is not achieved, decentralization is valuable because smaller states are *less able to exercise monopoly power than large states.*

Decentralization Brings Us Closer to Individual Political Independence

Rothbard noted that the purpose of seceding on the neighborhood level and beyond was to move toward true individual political independence:

> But, of course, if each person may secede from government, we have virtually arrived at the purely free society, where defense is supplied along with all other services by the free market and where the invasive State has ceased to exist.[7]

In this, Rothbard was not making a novel observation, but taking an argument earlier made by the *laissez-faire* economist Ludwig von Mises to its natural conclusion. In *Liberalism* (1927), Mises wrote of the need for highly localized government as a means of "self-determination." His view stemmed from the problem of ensuring that minority groups would not be overwhelmed by other groups that formed a majority within a larger jurisdiction. Mises writes:

> However, the right of self-determination of which we speak is not the right of self-determination of nations, but rather the right of self-determination of the inhabitants of every territory large enough to form an independent administrative unit. If it were in any way possible to grant this right of self-determination to every individual person, it would have to be done.[8]

---

[7]Ibid.

[8]Ludwig von Mises, *Liberalism: A Socio-Economic Exposition* (Kansas City, Mo.: Sheed Andrews and McMeel, 1962), p. 109.

Mises suggested that this could be accomplished through secession:

whenever the inhabitants of a particular territory, whether it be a single village, a whole district, or a series of adjacent districts, make it known, by a freely conducted plebiscite, that they no longer wish to remain united to the state to which they belong at the time, but wish either to form an independent state or to attach themselves to some other state, their wishes are to be respected and complied with.[9]

For his part, Mises apparently thought it too difficult—in terms of real-world implementation—to provide self-determination "to every individual person" even if separation was morally preferable.[10] Rothbard similarly regarded this sort of full-blown decentralization down to the individual as a difficult endeavor. Thus, he supported secession as a strategy which moved society in the proper *direction*:

---

[9]Ibid.

[10]Mises was surely familiar with the fact that plebiscites had already been used on numerous occasions to approve independence movements and the annexation of territories by larger states. By the beginning of the twentieth century, the idea of holding local elections to settle border disputes or the inclusion of a region within a certain polity was anything but novel. The use of plebiscites in this way dates back at least to the years of the French Revolution when the French state used plebiscites in the Papal States enclaves within France, and in other territories. Other examples include a 1905 plebiscite in which Norwegian voters approved secession from Sweden, and Iceland's independence plebiscite in 1919. For more examples from the nineteenth century, see Sarah Wambaugh, *A Monograph on Plebiscites: With a Collection of Official Documents* (New York: Carnegie Endowment for International Peace, 1920). Plebiscites have been used numerous times since Mises wrote these words, as well. For example, in 1964, Maltese voters approved independence from the United Kingdom in a plebiscite. In 1990, Slovenia declared independence from Yugoslavia via plebiscite. The new Slovenian republic ultimately won independence after the nearly bloodless Ten-Day War. In the wake of the collapse of the Soviet Union, plebiscites were held in several Soviet republics including Ukraine and the Baltic states. Outside Europe, of course, many more secession plebiscites were held throughout the twentieth century as part of the process of decolonization in Africa and Asia.

Pending total privatization, it is clear that our model could be approached, and conflicts minimized, by permitting secessions and local control, down to the micro-neighborhood level, and by developing contractual access rights for enclaves and exclaves. In the US, it becomes important, in moving toward such radical decentralization, for libertarians and classical liberals—indeed, for many other minority or dissident groups—to begin to lay the greatest stress on the forgotten Tenth Amendment and to try to decompose the role and power of the centralizing Supreme Court. Rather than trying to get people of one's own ideological persuasion on the Supreme Court, its power should be rolled back and minimized as far as possible, and its power decomposed into state, or even local, judicial bodies.[11]

This will strike many Americans as quite radical. Yet, for these theorists it is important to at least move in the direction of more localized control as a means of limiting state power and expanding individual prerogatives and choices. Like Mises, Rothbard contended that smaller, more decentralized government made it more likely that individuals would be able to live within a community that more closely reflected their individual preferences and needs. That is, secession is a tool to increase "self-determination" for both voluntary communities and individuals.

Smaller States Are Less Oppressive States

The second reason that Rothbard advocated secession and radical decentralization was his belief that small states were less capable of exercising power over those who lived within their borders.

As he noted in *Libertarian Forum*, Rothbard thought it a good thing that smaller states facilitated individual efforts to cross "the border to relatively greater freedom." Moreover, the smaller that states become, the less culturally isolated they are, and the less they are able to promote the myth that states can make their people better off through barriers to trade and exchange:

A common response to a world of proliferating nations is to worry about the multitude of trade barriers that might be

---

[11]Rothbard, "Nations by Consent."

erected. But, other things being equal, the greater the number of new nations, and the smaller the size of each, the better. For it would be far more difficult to sow the illusion of self-sufficiency if the slogan were "Buy North Dakotan" or even "Buy 56th Street" than it now is to convince the public to "Buy American." Similarly, "Down with South Dakota," or..."Down with 55th Street," would be a more difficult sell than spreading fear or hatred of the Japanese. Similarly, the absurdities and the unfortunate consequences of fiat paper money would be far more evident if each province or each neighborhood or street block were to print its own currency. A more decentralized world would be far more likely to turn to sound market commodities, such as gold or silver, for its money.[12]

It was this "greater competition between governments of different geographical areas" which Rothbard regarded as a net gain for individuals.

After all, as noted by historian Ralph Raico,[13] many economic historians by the mid-1970s had accepted the notion that competition between a large number of political units had been an important factor in Europe's rise to a region of relative material riches and relative political freedom. Historians E.L. Jones,[14] Jean Baechler,[15] and Douglass North[16] by the late seventies had all published new works contending that it was Europe's lack of a single dominant political entity—that is, Europe's relative "political anarchy"—which led to greater political freedom, and thus more economic prosperity.

---

[12]Ibid.

[13]Ralph Raico, "The Theory of Economic Development and the 'European Miracle'," in *The Collapse of Development Planning*, ed. Peter Boettke (New York: New York University Press, 1994), pp. 37–58.

[14]E.L. Jones, *The European Miracle* (Cambridge, U.K.: Cambridge University Press, 2003).

[15]Jean Baechler, *The Origins of Capitalism* (Oxford, U.K.: Basil Blackwell, 1975).

[16]Douglass North. "The Paradox of the West," in *The Origins of Modern Freedom in the West*, ed. R.W. Davis (Palo Alto, Calif.: Stanford University Press, 1995).

It is likely that Rothbard was aware of this, and in this recognized it as empirical support for what was in many ways common sense: a world of a multitude of states offers more options and more avenues of escape to those who face political oppression.

Later research has continued to support this position. Since the end of the Cold War, Europe's smaller states have been notable for being more open to free trade than larger states, and smaller states have pushed down their tax rates to attract capital. Indeed, the presence of this tax competition has pushed down tax rates in larger states as well. In Africa, too, smaller states have been shown to be more politically stable, more free, and less inclined toward controlled economies.

On both these counts, experience suggests that Rothbard has been right. For example, it's hard to see how Estonians, Poles, and Slovenians would all be somehow better off were they still chained to their old masters in Moscow or Belgrade. Meanwhile, experience continues to support the notion that it is small states and microstates that continue to offer freedom, choice, and openness of a sort not even contemplated by large states like China, or even Germany.

6

Nationalism as National Liberation: Lessons from the End of the Cold War

During the early 1990s, as the world of the old Soviet Bloc was rapidly falling apart, the economist and historian Murray Rothbard saw it all for what it was: a trend of mass decentralization and secession unfolding before the world's eyes. The old Warsaw Pact states of Poland, Hungary, and others won both *de jure* and *de facto* independence for the first time in decades. Other groups within the Soviet Union began to demand full blown *de jure* independence as well.

Rothbard approved of this, and he set to work encouraging the secessionists over the opposition of many foreign policy "experts."

"Nationalism" as Decentralization

For example, when it became clear in early 1990 that the Baltic states were preparing to secede from the rapidly fading Soviet state, the Soviets asked the West for help. As the *Los Angeles Times* noted at the time, "Soviet officials are stressing in their warnings...the danger of unleasing [*sic*] new and difficult-to-control forces through the separation of not only the Baltics but other Soviet republics."[1]

Unfortunately, the Bush administration expressed similar misgivings and the "'global democracy' establishment," as Rothbard called it, set to work trying to convince the world that these "nationalist" liberation movements were a threat to global peace.

The playbook then was similar to what it is now: "The concerns and demands of nationalities are dismissed as narrow, selfish, parochial, and even dangerously hostile *per se* and aggressive toward other nationalities."[2]

Thus, it was presumed that it was better for the Baltic-state nationalists to remain under Russian control and submit to the "democratic ideal." Rothbard summed up the endgame favored by the anti-nationalists:

> The Baltic nations…are "part" of the Soviet Union, and therefore their unilateral secession, against the will of the majority of the USSR, becomes an affront to "democracy," to "majority rule," and, last but far from least, to the unitary, centralizing nation-state that allegedly embodies the democratic ideal.[3]

Rothbard was forced to return to the topic in 1991, when Slovenia seceded from Yugoslavia in a nearly bloodless maneuver that led to a ten-day war with fewer than one hundred deaths. This all occurred, Rothbard noted, "despite the US and other powers moaning about the 'territorial integrity of Yugoslavia.'"[4]

Again in 1993, Rothbard had to defend secession for "national" groups when in late 1992, the Czechoslovakian state began talking

---

[1]Michael Parks, "Moscow Asks West's Help on Baltics: Soviet Union: The Kremlin wants U.S., other nations to discourage the region from seceding. A break could lead to a 'catastrophe,' a party official said," *Los Angeles Times*, January 15, 1990, https://www.latimes.com/archives/la-xpm-1990-01-15-mn-210-story.html.

[2]Murray N. Rothbard, "The Nationalities Question," in *The Irrepressible Rothbard* (Burlingame, Calif.: Center for Libertarian Studies, 2000), p. 227.

[3]Ibid. pp. 227–28.

[4]Murray Rothbard, "Welcome, Slovenia!," in *The Irrepressible Rothbard* (Burlingame, Calif.: Center for Libertarian Studies, 2000), pp. 238–41.

about breaking itself up into two countries.[5] Once again, the *New York Times* and other guardians of the "respectable" foreign policy establishment objected. When the separation finally took place, the *Times* was sure to run a one-sided editorial contending that the dissolution of the country was greeted with "wide regret" and ominously predicted that the move would add "new potential trouble spots to a Central Europe already convulsed by nationalism."[6]

Again and again, defenders of powerful centrally controlled states wrung their hands over the possibility that states might be broken up into smaller, independent, and more locally controlled pieces.

It should be noted that in all of these cases—from the Baltics to Prague, to Budapest and down to Slovenia—secession took place with very limited bloodshed, and certainly far less bloodshed than occurred under earlier communist strongmen. This, of course, is all studiously ignored today. Instead, national liberation is today denounced as "balkanization" and said to be synonymous with what happened in the *minority* of cases, namely, the bloodshed of the Yugoslav Wars.

In most cases, for all the warnings about Central Europe being "convulsed by nationalism," the fact remains that there were no massacres of Czechs by Slovakians, or *vice versa*. Outside Yugoslavia the travails suffered by ethnic minorities in the wake of the Soviet retreat were miniscule compared to what had been standard operating procedure under Soviet domination. The new Baltic ethnic majorities in the 1990s were not especially liberal toward the Russian-speaking minority, but in the nearly thirty years since the Baltic secessions, the Russian minorities have not been subjected to anything even approaching the same magnitude of terrors, killings, and Siberian deportation endured by the Baltic peoples under the Soviet state.

---

[5] Murray Rothbard, "Ex-Czechoslovakia," in *The Irrepressible Rothbard* (Burlingame, Calif.: Center for Liberian Studies, 2000), pp. 242–44.
[6] Stephen Engleberg, "Czechoslovakia Breaks In Two, to Wide Regret," *New York Times*, January 1, 1993.

Yet, had the foreign policy elites had their way thirty years ago Lithuanians, Estonians, and Latvians would still today be forced to live as a tiny minority under the Russian state. It's not hard to guess which way majority rule would go under those conditions. Yet democracy, we were told, would ensure that everything would turn out fine.

But, as Rothbard pointed out in 1994, in his essay "Nations by Consent," the pro-democracy, anti-secession party failed even on its own terms. After demanding respect for the territorial integrity of Yugoslavia (by then known as Serbia) the pro-democracy party ended up calling for secession after all:

> Take, for example, the current mess in Bosnia. Only a couple of years ago, Establishment opinion, Received Opinion of Left, Right, or Center, loudly proclaimed the importance of maintaining "the territorial integrity" of Yugoslavia, and bitterly denounced all secession movements. Now, only a short time later, the same Establishment, only recently defending the Serbs as champions of "the Yugoslav nation" against vicious secessionist movements trying to destroy that "integrity," now reviles and wishes to crush the Serbs for "aggression" against the "territorial integrity" of "Bosnia" or "Bosnia-Herzegovina," a trumped-up "nation" that had no more existence than the "nation of Nebraska" before 1991. But these are the pitfalls in which we are bound to fall if we remain trapped by the mythology of the "nation-state" whose chance boundary at time t must be upheld.[7]

The Logic of National Liberation

Although Rothbard returned to this issue in the 1990s because of the Soviet crack-up, his work in that period closely reflects his earlier writings on political independence movements.

Writing in September 1969, he frequently supported secession for the purpose of "national liberation," since "Aside from being a necessary condition to the achievement of justice, national liberation

---

[7]Murray N. Rothbard, "Nations by Consent," *The Journal of Libertarian Studies* 11, no. 1 (Fall 1994), https://mises.org/library/nations-consent.

is the only solution to the great world problems of territorial disputes and oppressive national rule."[8]

Rothbard supported the secession of Biafra from Nigeria in an editorial in 1970.[9] In 1977, he supported Quebecois nationalists, stating his hope that separatism and secession would lead to a "domino principle" in which secession would breed even *more* secession.[10]

It was very much in this line of thinking that Rothbard described the American Revolution as a case of national liberation:

> The American Revolution was radical in many other ways as well. It was the first successful war of national liberation against western imperialism. A people's war, waged by the majority of Americans having the courage and the zeal to rise up against constituted "legitimate" government, actually threw off their "sovereign." A revolutionary war led by "fanatics" and zealots rejected the siren calls of compromise and easy adjustment to the existing system.[11]

Not in this case or in any other case did Rothbard deny or ignore that there were those who ended up on the losing side as a result of secession. This was true of the Loyalists in America, of Russians in the Baltics, and of ethnic Serbs in Slovenia. But defending the mythical sanctity of the nation-state's *status quo* borders takes us down a road that is even more problematic. According to Rothbard, those who take this position "mistakenly scorn the idea of national liberation and independence as simply setting up more nation-states"—end up "becom[ing] in the concrete, objective supporters of the bloated, imperialistic nation-states of today."[12]

---

[8]Murray N. Rothbard, "National Liberation," *Egalitarianism as a Revolt Against Nature*, Second Edition (Auburn, Ala.: Mises Institute, 2000), p. 195.

[9]Murray N. Rothbard, "Biafra, RIP," *The Libertarian Forum*, February 1, 1970, p. 1.

[10]Murray N. Rothbard, "Vive Le Quebec Libre," *The Libertarian Forum*, January 1977, p. 8.

[11]Murray N. Rothbard, *Conceived in Liberty*, vol. 4, *The Revolutionary War, 1775–1784*, (Auburn, Ala.: Mises Institute, 1999), p. 443.

[12]Rothbard, "National Liberation," p. 195.

After all, if secession in the name of national liberation is bad, we end up on principle supporting the Soviet Union, and every empire or two-bit dictator who manages to hammer together a variety of disparate groups under a single national banner.

7

A Brief History of Secession Plebiscites in Europe

n the United States, the idea of a region of the country separating
through secession is generally regarded as an outrageously radical
and impractical move. Secession, it is often assumed, is obviously
beyond the pale of serious political discussion.

Yet, in spite of the US's (rather unwarranted) reputation for
expansive decentralization and local autonomy, we can find many
cases in which European regimes were far more willing to compromise on local assertions of autonomy and independence than is the
case in the United States.

Although fully or partially successful secession movements are
not *frequent* occurrences in Europe, we can nonetheless look to a
number of cases in which regions successfully carried forward independence movements at least to the point that a referendum was
held. In some of these cases, independence won voter approval and
was enacted.

Let's look at some of these cases to learn more.

Local Autonomy and Plebiscites
as a Component of Classical Liberalism

In his 1919 book, *Nation, State, and Economy*, Ludwig von Mises concludes that local independence is an assumed characteristic within a liberal (i.e., a "classically liberal" of "libertarian") polity. He writes:

> When a part of the people of the state wants to drop out of the union, liberalism does not hinder it from doing so. Colonies that want to become independent need only do so.... no people and no part of a people shall be held against its will in a political association that it does not want.

Moreover, in his 1927 book, *Liberalism: In the Classical Tradition*, Mises encourages the use of plebiscites in carrying this out. To some readers, this might seem a very radical position that Mises is taking. But, writing in the late teens and 1920s, Mises was working from what was becoming an established—albeit infrequently used—strategy for maintaining or increasing local autonomy within European states.

European Independence Plebiscites:
A Quick History

Perhaps the earliest uses of plebiscites to win local support for secession movements occurred in the late eighteenth century during the French Revolution. In an effort to enlarge the French state, plebiscites were used in the Papal States enclaves of Avignon and Comtat Venaissin in 1791, in Savoy in 1792, and in the Belgian Communes, Nice, and the Rhine Valley in 1793.[1]

In none of these cases was full independence contemplated, and these plebiscites only gave the voters a choice between the *status quo* and joining the French Republic. Nonetheless, pro-French sentiment was high in many of these areas and voters did indeed in many

---

[1]For an extensive description of nineteenth-century plebiscites, see Sarah Wambaugh, *A Monograph on Plebiscites: With a Collection of Official Documents* (New York: Carnegie Endowment for International Peace, 1920).

cases choose to secede from their status quo polities (i.e., the Papal States, Belgium, Sardinia) and join the French state.

By the nineteenth century, plebiscites were being increasingly used as part of the political process of changing which regime controlled certain districts and regions:

> [Plebiscites] were held in the transfer of control of Rome from the Papal State to Italy in 1870, in Denmark's sale of St. Thomas and St. John to the United States in 1868, and in Sweden's cession of St. Bartholomew to France in 1877.[2]

The Ionian Islands were transferred to Greece by Great Britain after the move was approved by voters in an 1863 plebiscite. Plebiscites were also used—beginning with the aftermath of the Treaty of Prague in 1866—in attempts to settle the so-called Schleswig question over the borderlands between Denmark and the German Confederation.

Secession in the Twentieth Century

By the beginning of the twentieth century, the idea of holding local elections to settle border disputes or the inclusion of a region within a certain polity was anything but novel.

In a 1905 plebiscite, nearly 100 percent of Norwegian voters approved dissolving Norway's union with Sweden. Norway became a fully independent state three months later.

In a 1918 plebiscite, Iceland's voters approved independence for the country in a personal union with Denmark under the Danish king. (The king would remain the head of state; Iceland became a republic after another plebiscite in 1944.)

In 1919, the Austrian region of Vorarlberg held a plebiscite to determine if the region should secede from Austria and join Switzerland as a new canton. Eighty-one percent of Vorarlberg voters approved the measure, but the movement failed due to opposition from the Swiss and Austrian governments, among others.

---

[2]Michael Hechter and Elizabeth Borland, "National Self-Determination: The Emergence of an International Norm," in *Social Norms*, eds. Michael Hechter and Karl-Dieter Opp (New York: Russell Sage Foundation, 2001), p. 193.

A plebiscite was held in Carinthia in October 1920 to resolve an ongoing border dispute between Yugoslavia and the new Austrian republic. Fifty-nine percent voted to attach Carinthia to Austria. In spite of opposition from Yugoslavian forces, the region ultimately became Austrian.

After World War I, several plebiscites were held as a means of implementing the Treaty of Versailles. These plebiscites, unlike locally driven plebiscites in, say, Vorarlberg and Iceland, were conducted under significant pressure from outside great powers—namely, the victorious Entente powers. Where plebiscites were actually held in German territory—such as in East Prussia—the results favored the Germans, but the Entente powers also simply transferred some areas of Germany to Poland and Czechoslovakia. (The Third Reich would later employ plebiscites in Austria and the Sudetenland as retribution for these territorial transfers.)

Plebiscites continued after the war in a much different post-war context. In 1946, a plebiscite was held to determine if the Faroe Islands should secede from Denmark. It narrowly failed. In 1955, voters in the Saar, a French protectorate, voted to join Germany. In 1964, Maltese voters approved independence from the United Kingdom in a plebiscite. In 1990, Slovenia declared independence from Yugoslavia via plebiscite. The new Slovenian republic ultimately won independence after the nearly bloodless Ten-Day War.

In the wake of the collapse of the Soviet Union, plebiscites were held in several Soviet republics including Ukraine and the Baltic states. (Outside Europe, of course, many more secession plebiscites were held throughout the twentieth century as part of the process of decolonization in Africa and Asia.)

Plebiscites in Perspective

As we can see from these examples, Mises's position in favor of plebiscites to implement self-determination plans through secession were not especially radical in the context of the late 1920s. After all, by the early twentieth century, they had come to be used as a tool for settling border disputes and as a means of allowing for local vetoes on international agreements involving attempts at changing which state controlled certain regions. In many cases, plebiscites did not offer the option of total independence, but provided an option to attach the region in question to a different sovereign state. But in some cases, plebiscites were used to establish the creation of new sovereign states such as Slovenia, Estonia, Iceland, and Norway. In many cases, the results of plebiscites were not carried out or were short lived even when implemented. For example, the Ionian Islands changed hands more than once after the 1863 vote.

But in most cases, plebiscites were employed to determine a question of secession, whether or not the end goal was ultimately full independence. In this, many have worked relatively well. In many cases, these plebiscites have helped to peacefully settle disputes and to send a message to central regimes about the prudence of granting independence to separatist regions that vote overwhelmingly for independence.

8

Why the US Supports Secession for Africans, but Not for Americans

The twentieth century was a century of secession. Since the end of the Second World War, the number of independent states in the world has nearly tripled as new states, through acts of secession, have come into existence. This was driven largely by the wave of decolonization that occurred following the Second World War.[1]

From the late 1940s through the 1970s, across Africa and Asia—and even in Europe, as in the case of Malta—dozens of colonial territories declared independence through referenda and other strategies. Throughout these processes of decolonization, much of the international community—including the United States—was supportive. Following the Second World War, the United States *explicitly* supported decolonization efforts, and was often quick to recognize the new countries' sovereignty and establish diplomatic relations.

---

[1] Alberto Alesina and Enrico Spolaore, "What's Happening to the Number and Size of Nations?" E-International Relations, November 9, 2015.

Th e U S f requently s upported t hese a cts o f s ecession, b ecause, it was said, it was morally imperative so as to respect the rights of "self-determination" denied to the world's colonized territories. Moreover, *many* of the world's sovereign states supported this global spree of secessionist movements, from the US to the Soviet Union and China, and within many international organizations like the United Nations. Yet when secession is suggested in *other* contexts, today's regimes are far less enthusiastic and generally condemn the very idea of secession.

For example, the Spanish regime today opposes independence for Catalonia and for the Basque Country. Th e R ussians f ought a long and bloody war to prevent independence for Chechnya. Th e U S regime would clearly take a very dim view of any member state or region that attempted to declare independence.

Doesn't this illustrate a glaring inconsistency in thinking? If self-determination is desirable for African or Asian colonies, why is secession *verboten* in other situations? Th e answer is it's easy to support secession in far-off territories of little strategic value. When secession hits "close to home," on the other hand, regimes that have long *pretended* to be in favor of self-determination will quickly turn on a dime and begin to manufacture a multitude of reasons as to why secession and self-determination are not, in fact, tolerable after all.

DefiningDo wn the Meaning of "Colony"

Th e idea of national self-determination a s a n e xplicit p olitical movement originates with the American Revolution. As Jefferson and his colleagues stated in the Declaration of Independence, "[I]t is the right of the people to alter or abolish" a government deemed to be abusive by the governed. Obviously—given that the Declaration of Independence was a declaration of secession—these strategies rightfully employed by "the people" included secession.

It is easy to apply Jeff erson's notion of self-determination to any colony, whether in North America in the eighteenth century or in Africa in the twentieth. Th us, governments looking to show off their humanitarian chops—what we might today call "virtue signaling"— will embrace secession. But *only* for purposes of decolonization—

and regimes are very careful to limit what they mean by "colonies" and "decolonization."

In this way of thinking, there's a clear line between a population oppressed by colonizers and one that isn't. Cases like Nigeria and India, for example, offer easy cases. Nigeria and India were both controlled by Britain and subject to British political domination. But, both these places are far away from Britain itself, and their populations—at least in the mid-twentieth century—were easy to distinguish visually from the British population. In other words, the people in these colonies "looked like" what one expects foreigners exploited by colonizers to look like. Moreover, these populations did not have direct representation in the British Parliament.

Yet none of these factors are really the key issues in determining if a population is denied self-determination. Yes, the Indians and the Nigerians did not have votes in Parliament. Yes, the Indians and the Nigerians often had interests very different from those of their rulers, who governed from thousands of miles away.

But colonization and the denial of self-determination is not just something that occurs in faraway lands where people look different and speak different languages.

In his 1927 book, *Liberalism*, Mises contends that the denial of self-determination is most certainly not just for people who live in colonial territories. Indeed, self-determination is routinely denied even *within* polities that are democratic. Mises writes:

> The situation of having to belong to a state to which one does not wish to belong is no less onerous if it is the result of an election than if one must endure it as the consequence of a military conquest....To be a member of a national minority always means that one is a second-class citizen.[2]

In other words, if a person, for whatever reason, is forced to be part of a nation-state or empire of which he does not wish to be a part— even if he can vote in elections—his situation is not fundamentally different from that of one who has been "colonized" via military conquest.

---

[2]Ludwig von Mises, *Liberalism: A Socio-Economic Exposition* (Kansas City, Mo.: Sheed Andrews and McMeel, 1962), p. 119.

After all, any group or any "people"—to use Jefferson's term—which is in a permanent voting minority will indeed find itself at an immense disadvantage. Mises illustrates this in the case of a person who is part of a linguistic minority:

> [W]hen he appears before a magistrate or any administrative official as a party to a suit or petition, he stands before men whose political thought is foreign to him because it developed under different ideological influences....At every turn the member of a national minority is made to feel that he lives among strangers and that he is, even if the letter of the law denies it, a second-class citizen.[3]

For Mises, the problem of linguistic minorities was the go-to example, but this framework can be applied to any number of other factors. Minority status could be based on religion, ethnicity, or ideology. Any "citizen" who finds himself within a group whose world view is substantially different from that of the ruling majority will be at a disadvantage.

That is, if a small minority group believes that circumcision is an important religious and cultural ritual but the majority vehemently believes circumcision is in fact barbaric, it is just a matter of time before the minority group's culture and religion will be gravely threatened.

In other words, this group will have been essentially colonized by the majority. It will be assimilated and subjected to the whims of what is a culturally alien power that just happens to be located geographically within the same community.

Limiting the Meaning of Self-Determination

Yet regimes are careful to ignore this problem or deny that colonized populations exist within the borders of the metropoles themselves. In their essay "National Self-Determination: The Emergence of an International Norm," Michael Hechter and Elizabeth Borland note the inconsistency, and how regimes create an arbitrary distinction between external colonies and internal ones:

---

[3]Ibid., pp. 119–20.

That culturally alien rule is deemed illegitimate in colonies but legitimate when it occurs within sovereign states (as in internal colonies) seems both logically and ethically inconsistent; but this is not necessarily so. Because decolonization does not tend to alter international boundaries, it does not directly threaten existing sovereign states. The secession of a region does cause a shift in international boundaries, however, and thus it represents a potential threat to the territorial integrity of many, if not most, extant states. This fact provides a political rationale for what otherwise appears to be a glaring inconsistency. Although few sovereign states, if any, might be prepared to endorse a principle that could threaten their own territorial integrity, a majority could (and did) vote for this *much more restrictive conception of self-determination*. (emphasis added)[4]

I think Hechter and Borland here err in concluding that the inconsistency has been overcome. It's still there. It's just that regimes have successfully managed to create the *impression* it's been overcome by creating an arbitrary distinction between varying types of colonies. So, when the United States regime conquered and annexed New Mexico and Hawaii, the regime was careful to define these as domestic noncolonial territories.

It's Not a Colony, It's the Homeland

The French did something similar with Algeria, although the strategy ultimately failed: as far as the French state was concerned, Algeria was not a colony, but was an "integral part of France." After 1848, Algeria was designed to become like any other French region, complete with representation in the national legislature. Thus, France fought hard against Algerian independence both in Algeria itself and in international forums like the United Nations. France insisted that the loss of Algeria would mean the loss of core French territory.

The situation was similar in the American Southwest. The only difference is that Anglo-American settlers eventually overwhelmed

---

[4]Michael Hechter and Elizabeth Borland, "National Self-Determination: The Emergence of an International Norm," in *Social Norms*, eds. Michael Hechter and Karl-Dieter Opp (New York: Russell Sage Foundation, 2001), p. 199.

both the Mexican and indigenous populations in New Mexico, thus ensuring that the colonized populations could never hope to assert independence or autonomy.

Indeed, the arbitrariness of regimes' limited conception of self-determination is all the more highlighted by the presence and plight of indigenous populations within settler-majority nations (e.g., Canada, the US, Argentina, Mexico).

In these cases, we find many groups that are still characterized by culture and language that is separate from that of the majority population. Moreover, these groups are often even tied to specific geographic areas. In the US, for instance, we see this with "native American" populations on tribal lands.

Yet the US regime is careful to never refer to these tribal lands as "colonies" or colonized areas although that is clearly what they are. As suggested by Hechter and Borland, the reason lies in the fact that to label these areas as colonies would give fuel to the notion that, as with African and Asian colonies, these areas deserve self-determination either through full secession or at least through a radical shift toward regional autonomy. To do so would present a threat to the "territorial integrity" of the US itself.

Democracy Will Fix It!

So, it is not surprising that today's regimes reject the notion that denial of self-determination is even *possible* along the lines laid out by Mises. If a religious, ethnic, or ideological group finds itself in the minority, regimes insist that self-determination can nonetheless be achieved through democracy within the political forms preferred by regimes. This is not a realistic hope for groups that are in a state of permanent minority, however.

Although Western regimes like the United States like to talk a lot about self-determination for others outside the US itself, the regime and its supporters steadfastly deny that the nation contains any minority groups—ideological, religious, or otherwise—that ought to be granted autonomy in the fashion of colonized populations in Africa or Asia. Even when the Left emphasizes the existence of "oppressed minorities" the answer always lies in a larger, more active regime, and in promises of more democracy.

9

From Taxes to Trade, More Secession Means More Freedom

When we hear of political movements in favor of decentralization and secession, the word "nationalist" is often used to describe them. We have seen the word used in both the Scottish and Catalonian secession movements, and in the case of Brexit. Often the term is intended to be pejorative.

When used pejoratively—as by the critics of Brexit—the implication is that the separatists seek to exit a larger political entity for the purposes of increasing isolation, throwing up greater barriers to trade, and pursuing a more autarkic economic policy. In other words, we're supposed to believe that efforts at decentralizing political systems leads to states becoming more oppressive and more protectionist.

But there's a problem with this claim, and with connecting protectionist nationalism to decentralization and secession: the act of breaking up political bodies into smaller pieces works *contrary* to the supposed goals of nationalism.

That is, when a political jurisdiction is broken up into smaller independent units, those new units are likely to become *more* reliant on economic integration and trade, not less. This dependency increases as the country size becomes smaller. If the goals of the nationalists include economic autarky and isolation, nationalists will quickly find these goals very hard to achieve indeed.[1]

This is true for at least three reasons.

One:
Economic Self-Sufficiency Is Costly and Difficult

Economic self-sufficiency—i.e., autarky—has long been a dream of protectionists. The idea here is that the population within a given state benefits when the residents of that state can cut themselves off from other states while still maintaining a high standard of living. Fueled by the false notion that imports represent economic losses for an economy, protectionists seek policies that block or minimize the importation of foreign goods.

Large countries can pull this off—for a little while. For countries with vast agricultural hinterlands, large industrial cities, and innovative service sectors, it is possible to move toward economic reliance on only domestic foodstuff, domestic raw materials, and domestic industry.

Over time, however, protectionist states begin to fall behind the rest of the world, which is presumably still engaging in international trade. It will become increasingly clear that the protectionist states are not keeping up in terms of their standards of living. This will

---

[1] The use of the UK as an example here is primarily based on the fact it has moved from a larger borderless confederation (i.e., the EU) to a position as an independent state with much less direct access to a single market. Overall, for our purposes here, the UK can only be described as a "smaller" state and economy (compared to the EU), but not as a "small country." "Small" is a term best reserved for countries that are significantly smaller than the large European states of Germany, the UK, France, Italy, and Spain. This would arguably include the Netherlands (with approximately 25 million in population) but would definitely include Switzerland (with 8 million residents) and other states of similar size. And then there are the "microstates" (e.g., Luxembourg, Liechtenstein) with populations under one million.

have geopolitical implications as well, since protectionist countries will become relatively impoverished and relatively less innovative compared to other states. Protectionist states thus lose relative power both economically and militarily.

We saw this at work in Latin America, for instance, when it was in the thrall of dependency theory during the mid-twentieth century. The idea was that countries could become wealthier and more politically independent by reducing trade. The strategy failed. Geopolitically, the isolationist regimes of Asia set themselves back decades through their attempts to achieve autarky.

The process is the same with small countries, but the effects of protectionism become more apparent more quickly. After all, an autarkic small country that lacks a diverse economy or a large agricultural sector will quickly find itself running out of food, skilled labor, and raw materials. Moreover, a small country without close economic ties to other nations will also soon find itself in a very dangerous geopolitical position.

Perhaps not surprisingly, empirical studies have found that small countries tend to be more open to international trade than larger countries. In their study of small economies, Sergio Castello and Terutomo Ozawa found

> Small economies, when economically successful and compared to their larger counterparts, tend to be: more export focused in manufacturing, likely to specialize in differentiated manufactures, more actively involved with direct overseas businesses…[and] more actively involved in international trade through varying degrees of economic integration.[2]

These realities have not been lost on those who control these small states, and small regimes have enthusiastically sought out more opportunities to engage in international trade.[3] Castello and Ozawa conclude that in a world of specialized and growing trade:

---

[2]Sergio Castello and Terutomo Ozawa, *Globalization of Small Economies as a Strategic Behavior in International Business* (New York: Routledge, 1999), p. xii.

[3]Openness on the part of small states is not limited only to recent decades. A 1960 study by Simon Kuznets, "Economic Growth of Small Nations," in

Small economies naturally grow more trade-oriented in both exports and imports...Ceteris paribus, small nations thus become more trade-focused than large ones.[4]

Indeed, this may be the *only* way for them to prosper. As Gary Becker noted during the period when new post-Soviet states were entering the global marketplace:

Small nations are proliferating because economies can prosper by producing niche goods and services for world markets....In fact, small nations now have advantages in the competition for international markets. Economic efficiency requires them to concentrate on only a few products and services, so they often specialize in niches that are too small for large nations to fill.[5]

Small countries can't offer the world a wide variety of goods and services, but they can specialize and offer at least *some* goods or services for which there is global demand. Without doing this, small states have little hope of raising their standards of living. This is why economists Enrico Spolaore and Alberto Alesina concluded in 1995 that "smaller countries will need more economic integration" in order to benefit from independence.[6]

This all suggests that the need to integrate becomes greater the smaller the state, and that the need for economic openness and integration are even greater for microstates—the smallest of the small

---

Robinson (1960) "does find a substantial difference in terms of openness to trade in the sample of the 30 richest countries he considers: small countries were more open to trade than large ones among the world's richest countries in 1949." Quoted in "Economic consequences of the size of nations, 50 years on" by Eloi Laurent. Published by HAL archives-ouvertes, https://hal-sciencespo. archives-ouvertes.fr/hal-00972823/document.

[4]Ibid., p. 26.

[5]Paul J.J. Welfens, David B. Audretsch, John T. Addison, Hariolf Grupp, *Technological Competition, Employment and Innovation Policies in OECD Countries* (Berlin: Springer-Verlag, 1998), p. 98.

[6]Alberto F. Ades and Edward L. Glaeser, "Trade and Circuses: Explaining Urban Giants," Working Paper No. 4715, National Bureau of Economic Research. April 1994, https://www.nber.org/system/files/working_papers/w4715/w4715.pdf.

states. William Easterly and Aart Kraay found in 1999, for example, that in spite of the "widely held view that small states suffer from their openness," financial "openness may help microstates insure against the large shocks they receive." This is in part due to the fact that financial openness "allows countries to share risks with the rest of the world."[7]

The impetus for small states to pursue open trade policies exists even in the presence of potentially threatening larger states. In his study of how trade is affected by state size, Stephen Krasner notes that

> Small states are likely to opt for openness because the advantages in terms of aggregate income and growth are so great, and their political power is bound to be restricted regardless of what they do.[8]

Two:
Smaller Countries Seek Tax Competition
and Tax Arbitrage

Trade isn't the only place where small states look to lessen regulatory burdens and tax burdens.

Smaller states also have a habit of competing with larger states by lowering tax rates. As recounted by Gideon Rachman in the *Financial Times*, numerous small states were integrating into the European economy in the late 1990s and early 2000s. According to Rachman:

> Small and nimble nations slashed taxes and regulation to attract foreign capital and business. The Irish set some of the lowest corporation tax rates in Europe; the Balts and Slovaks went for flat taxes; Iceland became an improbable financial centre. International capital flooded into the smalls.[9]

---

[7]William Easterly, and Aart Kraay, "Small States, Small Problems?" June 1, 1999, www.ssrn.com/abstract_id=620631.

[8]Stephen D. Krasner, "State Power and the Structure of International Trade," *World Politics* 28, no. 3 (April, 1976): 317–47 and 322, http://rochelleterman. com/ir/sites/default/files/krasner%201976.pdf.

[9]"How small nations were cut adrift" *Financial Times*, October 19, 2009, https:// www.ft.com/content/e2da4314-bcda-11de-a7ec-00144feab49a.

Did this mean that smaller states in general—at least those with easy access to Europe—tended to embrace lower tax rates? The answer appears to be yes. In a 2012 study, author Franto Ricka concludes "capital tax rates in the EU countries are positively related to their size partly because small countries choose a lower tax on capital than larger countries, with which they compete."[10] While large states can rely on economies of scale to keep capital from defecting in response to tax increases, small states have no such advantage. Thus, small states must be, as Ricka puts it "tougher competitors for scarce capital."[11] Moreover, Ricka found that the presence of small countries—and the tax competition they created—drove down tax rates in the larger countries.

Not surprisingly, large states have attempted to pressure small states into raising tax rates and embracing so-called tax harmonization. In early 2019, for example, European Commission president Jean-Claude Juncker pushed the idea of ending the ability of EU members to veto changes in tax policy so as to make tax rates across EU countries more equal.[12] The relatively small states of Ireland and Hungary have long opposed such efforts.[13] Malta has vehemently objected as well.[14] Europe isn't the only place with small states looking to attract capital with low tax rates. Small island nations in

---

[10]Franto Ricka, "The right-wing power of small countries," Working Paper No. 153, Prepared in December 2012, European Bank for Reconstruction and Development, https://www.ebrd.com/downloads/research/economics/workingpapers/wp0153.pdf.

[11]Ibid., p. 2.

[12]Alex Barker, "Brussels pushes to end national vetoes on taxation," January 14, 2019, *The Irish Times*, https://www.irishtimes.com/business/economy/brussels-pushes-to-end-national-vetoes-on-taxation-1.3757137.

[13]"Hungary, Ireland oppose EU-wide tax harmonization efforts" by Reuters Staff, January 4, 2018, https://www.reuters.com/article/us-hungary-ireland-taxation/hungary-ireland-oppose-eu-wide-tax-harmonization-efforts-idUSKBN1ET1ZY.

[14]"No EU tax harmonization anytime soon-European Commission vice-president," *Malta Today*, March 5, 2019, https://www.maltatoday.com.mt/news/europe/93408/watch_no_eu_tax_harmonisation_anytime_soon__european_commission_vicepresident#.YEpuSbCSmUm.

the Caribbean also function as tax havens and have earned the ire of the European Union's leadership.[15]

When it comes to tax rates, it's the large states—and especially unions of large states like the EU—that are the drivers behind efforts to raise taxes worldwide. The efforts threaten to end the havens offered by smaller states looking to attract capital that would likely ignore small states otherwise.

Three:
Small States Actually Perform Better

Finally, as an added motivation to small states to lower trade barriers and tax rates, there is the empirical evidence showing that small states can achieve higher growth rates and higher standards of living through more liberal economic policy.

Economist Gary Becker in 1998 noted, "since 1950 real per capita GDP has risen somewhat faster in smaller nations than it has in bigger ones."[16] Becker concluded that "the statistics on actual performance show that dire warnings about the economic price suffered by small nations are not all warranted….Smallness can be an asset in the division of labor in the modern world, where economies are linked through international transactions."[17] Of the fourteen countries with populations over 100 million, only the US and Japan are wealthy.[18]

---

[15]Daniel Boffey, "In wake of Brexit, EU to put Cayman Islands on tax haven blacklist," *The Guardian*, February 13, 2020, https://www.theguardian.com/us-news/2020/feb/13/eu-to-put-cayman-islands-on-tax-haven-blacklishttps://www.theguardian.com/us-news/2020/feb/13/eu-to-put-cayman-islands-on-tax-haven-blacklist.

[16]Gary S. Becker, Guity Nashat Becket, *The Economics of Life: From Baseball to Affirmative Action to Immigration, How Real-World Issues Affect Our Everyday Life* (New York: McGraw Hill Professional, 1997), p. 282.

[17]Castello and Ozawa, *Globalization of Small Economies as a Strategic Behavior in International Business*, p. 90.

[18]Roger Kerr, "The Size of Nations," *New Zealand Business Roundtable*, February 2, 2005, http://www.scoop.co.nz/stories/BU0502/S00021.htm.

Moreover, Easterly and Kraay write: "controlling for location, smaller states are actually richer than other states in per capita GDP….microstates have on average higher income and productivity levels than small states, and grow no more slowly than large states," the only "penalty of smallness" being relatively higher GDP growth rates volatility due to trade exposure.[19]

Nor are the indicators favoring small states based only on numbers like income and productivity.[20] Nick Slater, in an article titled "Every State Should be a Microstate" observes

> [People] tend to live longer [in microstates]: out of the top ten countries in terms of life expectancy, nine could be considered microstates (of these, Switzerland is a bit of a stretch, but its population is still smaller than New York City's). It can also be good for your bank account: the quality of life in European microstates like Luxembourg, Liechtenstein, and San Marino is perhaps the highest in the world.[21]

Smallness brings other intangible benefits as well. Legal scholar F.H. Buckley notes that small northern European countries tend to be exceptionally wealthy and healthy. But Buckley asserts this isn't a product of these countries' alleged (and much vaunted) socialism. Rather the empirical evidence suggests these countries are notable for their economic and political stability because they have small populations with a high degree of social cohesion. As just one example, Buckley notes Finland—with a population of under 6 million, is:

---

[19]Easterly and Kraay, "Small States, Small Problems?"

[20]A 2014 report from Credit Suisse titled "The Success of Small Countries" concludes: "If we add education, healthcare or intangible infrastructure as measures of success, we find that small countries do proportionately very well. For example, with respect to UN's Human Development Index (which combines GNI per capita, education and health metrics), small countries make up over half of the world's top 30 countries," https://www.ara.cat/2014/08/05/1187961194.pdf?hash=f2b1f4ba8c1b6bd92a473d05791bfb8fdad50e60.

[21]Nick Slater, "Every State Should be a Microstate" *Current Affairs*, August 9, 2019.

one of the richest and least corrupt countries in the world. It also has the kind of social cohesion and unity that only small countries can have….If the country were twenty times bigger, it would be more diverse and less unified. Its leaders would be more remote from the people, and their policies more tainted by interest group corruption.[22]

Many countries have economic and political systems like Finland and Denmark and Norway. But these places are remarkable for their smallness and lack of diversity—and thus lack of competing linguistic, socio-economic and ethnic groups—within the population. Buckley concludes that bigness is not *necessarily* an obstacle to relative safety, prosperity, and social cohesion. But bigness doesn't help.

Now, this isn't to say that smallness is a foolproof strategy for economic success. There's a reason Easterly and Kraay control for location in their comparisons. Other research suggests that small and remote countries tend to be uncompetitive.[23]

But even in Africa, small states outperformed large states in economic growth. According to a 2007 report from the World Bank, the resilience of small states was likely due to the greater economic flexibility observed in them, and thanks to political stability. This stability, it is believed, stemmed in part from the fact that smaller African countries are less "ethnically fractionalized."[24]

Unilateralism Doesn't Mean Protectionism

All too often, opponents of decentralization and secession insist that whenever a region, member state, or nation is allowed to go its own way, it will immediately raise trade barriers, raise taxes, and forget the benefits of international cooperation. Yet, in recent decades, there

---

[22]F.H. Buckley, *American Secession* (New York: Encounter Books, 2020), p. 63.
[23]Admir Čavalić, "Economic Freedom and Development of Small Countries, *Acta Economica* 15, no. 27 (2017), http://ae.ef.unibl.org/index.php/AE/article/view/60.
[24]Dörte Dömeland and Frederico Gil Sander, "Growth in African Small States," April 2007, https://www.academia.edu/4391207/Growth_in_African_Small_States.

is scant evidence to suggest that this is a likely outcome in practice. It appears far more likely that seceding countries and territories will move in the opposite direction of these dire predictions: away from economic nationalism and toward a more open economy.

10

If California Secedes, What Happens to Locals Who Opposed Secession?

I n recent years, left-wing groups have often been the driving force behind secession movements. This has been the case in Scotland, in Catalonia, and in California.

In each case, the secession movements have been initiated in part to forward left-wing goals, such as the creation of a larger welfare state or to escape limitations imposed by political interest groups and institutions deemed to be too right-wing.

Within the American context, the loudest calls for secession during the Trump years were coming from California where leftists were eager to assert their independence from the administration in Washington. Generally speaking, these California secessionists wanted single-payer health care, an even larger welfare state, confiscation of private firearms, and an ever larger environmental "protection" bureaucracy. That is, they wanted a European-style welfare state.

California as Case Study

This case presented Americans—and especially libertarian-minded Americans—with a question that continues to come up in recent years on secession matters: should one support a secession movement that seeks ideological goals contrary to one's own positions? Specifically, in the case of free-market liberal activists, the question is whether or not one ought to support secession movements seeking more interventionist government.

The answer must first and foremost be compared against the reality of forcing political union on a separatist region. That is, the cost of allowing a region to separate must be compared to the cost of keeping it in—i.e., military invasion, occupation, mass arrests, government surveillance, martial law, and worse.

Not surprisingly, we're forced to conclude the answer is the same whether we're talking about secession in Scotland, in California, or in Catalonia: using the force of the state to oppose secessionist movements is generally both immoral and impractical. After all, if a region—say, California—votes in the majority to secede, to prevent secession ultimately comes down to the use of physical force to ensure "unity." This, of course, is contrary to the very idea of self-determination.

What About the Minority Interests?

Nonetheless, those who oppose secession in these cases point to those groups in the minority who continue to reside in the seceding territories.

The argument goes something like this: "Now that you've cut California loose, what about those poor conservatives, gun owners, and business owners who will now be negatively impacted by a newly empowered California government? Before, California was at least somewhat restrained by its membership in the United States. Now, the California government is even more free to inflict misery on the hapless taxpayers and productive people who are stuck there."

To this criticism, there are at least two responses.

One:
California Independence Means More Freedom
for the Rest of the Country

Those who wish to focus on merely what happens to those who are in California take a parochial and far-too-limited view. Yes, it's true that business owners, religious Christians, and gun owners in California (to name just three groups) would likely be negatively impacted by California independence. California's ruling regime has long shown an open hostility to these minority groups.

The other side of the coin, however, is that California secession would lead to a significant expansion of freedom for the "rump" United States left behind. Freed of the influence of California on American politics, the remainder of the United States would likely move significantly in the direction of *more* freedom in markets. Federal regulations would likely be scaled back, and presidential candidates would no longer need to cater to interest groups with sizable influence in California.

California's 53-member delegation in Congress would be gone, and voting patterns in Congress would likely shift in a direction more hospitable to *laissez-faire.*

In other words, the nation would be freed from a great weight tied around its neck. One might even say the situation is analogous to the removal of an infected appendage. It wouldn't be the first time such a thing had happened. In 1861, when Southern States began seceding from the Union, New Yorker George Templeton Strong welcomed the prospect of being freed from the political influence of the slavedrivers down south. He concluded "the self-amputated members were diseased beyond immediate cure, and their virus will infect our system no longer."[1]

But, unlike Strong who might have been induced by conscience to think of the slaves left behind in the seceding territories, we face no similar problem. Obviously, comparing modern California to a slave state of old is absurd, and unlike the slaves, Californians are

---

[1] George Templeton Strong, *The Diary of George Templeton Strong* (New York: Macmillan, 1952), p. 94.

free to move away. Nor is it the moral obligation of Texans, or Floridians, or Coloradans to protect the Californians from the excesses of their own government.

Thus, when we think of post-secession California subject to the whims of a leftist government there, we must also think of the 285 million remaining Americans who would benefit from the separation.

Note also that this situation even has advantages for the taxpayers and business owners in California who wish to escape the California regime.

Now that the rump United States has been improved by California's absence, those in California who seek a more business-friendly legal environment can dramatically change their fortunes for the better by moving across the new national boundary to Arizona or Nevada. For these migrants, the net gain achieved by leaving California has grown larger thanks to California's departure.

Two:
More States Are Preferable to Fewer States

The second response to the objection lies in the fact that secession already brings with it a solution to the problem. That is, the problems caused by one secession are solved by *more* secession.

A larger number of states is preferable to a smaller number. A larger number of small states provides more practical choices to taxpayers and citizens in choosing a place to live under governments that more closely match their personal values.

Thus, in considering the problems of an independent California, we find that the primary problem faced by taxpayers and productive residents in California is that the state is simply too large and contains too diverse a population within its boundaries.

As noted by numerous commentators over the years—including supporters of the Six Californias initiative—California's population is quite politically and culturally diverse, although it has been dominated for decades by a coalition of center-left voters based around the Bay Area. Compared to these voters, Southern California residents appear moderately conservative but one would not know this by looking at statewide politics because Northern California is so adept at throwing its weight around.

The solution to this problem lies in breaking up California into still smaller pieces. We can see many of these political lines ripe for decentralization in the voting patterns revealed by statewide votes such as those for Proposition 187 and Proposition 8.[2] We can see it in the map of legislative districts. Nor is this just a matter of metropolitan areas versus rural areas. Many suburban areas within the metroplexes of California are quite right-of-center in their own rights, and would surely benefit from further political decentralization.

Urban core cities ought to be their own self-governing territories, with suburban and rural areas kept separate and self-governing in their own ways.[3]

The net result of all of this would be to offer a multitude of choices among taxpayers, entrepreneurs, gun owners, and moral traditionalists as to where they might live and enjoy the benefits of self-determination within their own communities.

But before any of this can happen, we must first establish and extend the moral and legal legitimacy of self-determination through secession and decentralization. Clinging to the status quo of existing regional and national boundaries is reactionary in the extreme. Insisting that no community ought to be allowed

---

[2]At least as late as 2008, California was not nearly as ideologically uniform as the popular narrative suggested. For example, Proposition 8 was a 2008 California ballot measure that banned government sanctioned same-sex marriage in the state. It passed with 52 percent of the vote, with even a majority of voters in Los Angeles County voting to ban government-sanctioned gay marriage. A similar phenomenon occurred with Proposition 187 in 1994. That ballot measure—which was designed to curb illegal immigration, and thus considered "conservative" legislation—passed with 58 percent of the vote, and won majorities in Los Angeles, Orange, and San Diego counties.

[3]For a model of local self-determination within the existing US state-local framework, see Ryan McMaken, "Grant Statehood to America's Core Cities," *Mises Wire,* August 29, 2017, https://mises.org/blog/give-sanctuary-cities-what-they-want.

self-determination unless its leaders agree with us in nearly every respect is impractical, irresponsible, and doomed to failure.

Nevertheless, when confronted with new attempts at decentralization and secession, even some of those who claim to be for freedom and self-determination cling to ideas of imposing nationalistic control over others. They invent emotion-laden fictional slogans claiming "we are one nation" or "secession is treason" or other sayings designed to justify using the power of the state to impose political unity. Ultimately, this is an ideology of monopoly and coercion, and tramples the very ideals of freedom that the nationalists claim they hold dear.

11

How Small Is Too Small?

O nly hours after the final results came in for a British exit from the EU, political leaders in Scotland were talking about renewing their drive to secede from the United Kingdom.[1] Pointing to the fact that a large majority of Scots voted to remain in the EU during the Brexit vote, Scottish advocates for independence are now claiming (convincingly) that many Scots are leaving the EU against their will.

Many of us who advocated for Scottish secession in 2014 were, of course fine with Scottish secession at the time. And we're still fine with it now. Scotland should be free to say good bye and go its own way.

Some opponents of Scottish exit, however, have claimed that Scotland is too small "to go it alone." Defenders of Scottish independence call this the "too wee, too poor, too stupid" argument.

Even the most rudimentary analysis, however, shows that its relatively small size hardly renders Scotland an outlier among independent states. With an estimated nominal GDP of approximately

---

[1]"Brexit: Nicola Sturgeon says second Scottish independence vote 'highly likely'," *BBC News*, June 24, 2016, https://www.bbc.com/news/uk-scotland-scotland-politics-36621030.

$205 billion, Scotland's total output is not much different from Greece and New Zealand. Scotland's economy is larger than that of both Hungary ($163 billion) and Iceland ($24 billion).

With a population of 5.3 million, this puts Scotland either similar to, or larger than, Denmark, Norway, Finland, New Zealand, and Ireland. With a population this size, Scotland's GDP per capita comes out to around $38,000 which naturally is somewhat similar to the UK overall ($41,000), and also similar to France ($40,300) and Japan ($40,100). Scotland's GDP per capita well exceeds Italy's GDP per capita of $33,100.

Some will argue that Scots cannot go it alone because they rely too much on English taxpayers for transfer payments such as pensions. This is no doubt partially true, although the UK government also extracts tax dollars from Scots, and regulates Scottish trade with the EU and everyone else. It is possible that many residents of Scotland would desire independence even if it means a temporary disruption in living standards.

Overall, though, there's no denying that Scotland, even by itself, is well within the realm of ordinary wealthy nation states, in terms of population, and the size of its economy. Scotland is not an impoverished outlier.

The claim that it is "too small" was repeated, however, in a December 2013 article by Roger Bootle at *The Telegraph* in which he writes:

> Believe it or not, there is an extensive economic literature on the subject of the optimum size of a country, or more accurately, political association. From the economic point of view, as the size of political entities gets larger, there is scope for economies of scale in government and the provision of public goods such as defence. Equally, within a single political entity there are no restrictions on trade, such as tariffs or quotas so, other things being equal, the gains from trade are maximised as political entities grow larger.
>
> Yet there are limits to the desirable size of political entities, such that, as things stand anyway, a single world government would not be optimal. The larger, and certainly the more heterogeneous, a political entity is, the more resources are taken up with arguing about distribution, that is to say who should benefit from

various sorts of public expenditure, and who should pay for it. The quality of government tends to deteriorate.[2]

Bootle is correct that there are certainly advantages of size when it comes to national defense. Obviously, it's much harder for a foreign invader to overrun Russia than Poland. What Bootle misses, however, is that these issues can be addressed through confederation rather than through unitary political institutions. The original purpose of the United States, of course, was to act as a confederation for purposes of national defense. Member states however—for a time—remained autonomous within their own borders. Similar structures have existed throughout history, from NATO to the Hanseatic league of northern Europe.

Scotland need not be part of the UK to enter into a defense agreement with the English.

The rest of Bootle's argument appears even more specious. It is not a given, for example, that larger states facilitate trade. As the UK experience has shown, membership in the EU has granted access to *some* markets, but it has cut off access and flexibility with other markets. (Norway and Switzerland have access to these same markets, by the way, without EU membership.)

This was also an enormous issue and source of conflict in the United States in regards to southern states. Yes, membership in the United States facilitated trade among states, but during the nineteenth century, trade between Southern states and foreign markets was hampered by US tariff policy.

In fact, there are many reasons to believe that the "optimal" size of a state is considerably smaller than what Bootle suggests it is. (The subtext of Bootle's article, of course, is that Scotland is below the optimal size.) As Peter St. Onge wrote in 2014 about the Scottish referendum at the time:

---

[2]Roger Bootle, "Scotland may prefer to go it alone, but the EU has lessons for countries that secede," *The Telegraph*, December 1, 2013, https://www.telegraph. co.uk/finance/comment/rogerbootle/10487194/Scotland-may-prefer-to-go-it-alone-but-the-EU-has-lessons-for-countries-that-secede.html.

So small is possible. But is it a good idea?

The answer, perhaps surprisingly, is resoundingly "Yes!" Statistically speaking, at least. Why? Because according to numbers from the World Bank Development Indicators, among the 45 sovereign countries in Europe, small countries are nearly twice as wealthy as large countries. The gap between biggest-10 and smallest-10 ranges between 84 percent (for all of Europe) to 79 percent (for only Western Europe).

This is a huge difference: To put it in perspective, even a 79 percent change in wealth is about the gap between Russia and Denmark. That's massive considering the historical and cultural similarities especially within Western Europe.

Even among linguistic siblings the differences are stark: Germany is poorer than the small German-speaking states (Switzerland, Austria, Luxembourg, and Liechtenstein), France is poorer than the small French-speaking states (Belgium, Andorra, Luxembourg, and Switzerland again and, of course, Monaco). Even Ireland, for centuries ravaged by the warmongering English, is today richer than their former masters in the United Kingdom, a country fifteen times larger.

Why would this be? There are two reasons. First, smaller countries are often more responsive to their people. The smaller the country the stronger the policy feedback loop. Meaning truly awful ideas tend to get corrected earlier. Had Mao Tse Tung been working with an apartment complex instead of a country of nearly a billion-people, his wacky ideas wouldn't have killed millions.

Second, small countries just don't have the money to engage in truly crazy ideas. Like Wars on Terror or world-wide daisy-chains of military bases. An independent Scotland, or Vermont, is unlikely to invade Iraq. It takes a big country to do truly insane things.[3]

A Lesson for American States

When Americans indulge in thought experiments about the possible secession of American states, it is often assumed that most US member states are too small "to go it alone." Indeed, most Americans

[3]Peter St. Onge, "Is Scotland Big Enough To Go it Alone?" *Mises Daily,* September 11, 2014, https://mises.org/library/scotland-big-enough-go-it-alone.

greatly underestimate the size of many American member states in relation to numerous independent and prosperous foreign states.

Were Scotland a US member state, for example, it would be only a medium-sized state, with a GDP smaller than the gross state products of both Oregon and Alabama, making it about the 25th largest state in terms of GDP. Population-wise, Scotland is about equal to Minnesota and Colorado.

Moreover, few Americans appreciate how enormous some American states are, especially the largest four states: California, Texas, New York, and Florida.

In terms of both population and GDP, California is about equal to Canada—and with much better weather. Texas is equal in economy and population size to Australia. Pennsylvania's economy is similar in size to Switzerland.

Even America's smaller and less wealthy member states tend to be large and wealthy in international comparisons. Missouri has a larger economy than Ireland and Finland. Ohio has a larger economy than both Argentina and Norway.

While secession of American states is often dismissed as absurd, there are few reasons to believe that a state like Texas—to name just one example—could not immediately transition from American member state to sovereign nation-state. With a large economy, port cities, oil, and easy access to European, Latin American, and even Asian economies by sea, economic arguments against such a separation fall flat. And of course, the success of smaller states like Norway, Denmark, and Switzerland illustrate that bigness is truly unnecessary. Naturally, many other states even beyond the biggest states—such as Pennsylvania, New Jersey, North Carolina, Ohio and others—could do the same. These states would all be among the world's polities with the largest economies were they independent countries.

"But what about national defense!" some may argue. "Wouldn't Texas be constantly at war with the United States?" Experience suggests that Texas would be at war with the United States about as frequently as Canada has been at war with the United States: zero times since 1815. International wars rarely erupt between countries with common languages, common histories, and common economic interests. Should Scotland secede, the UK won't be sending in the tanks, and Scotland could easily join the realm of independent nation states, just as many American states could do the same.

12

When It Comes to National Defense, It's More than Size that Matters

I
n the debate over whether or not China will soon rise to challenge the United States as the world's hegemon, it is often assumed that states with large aggregate economies are necessarily more militarily powerful ones. This assumption is then used to argue that the West, and the United States in particular, must support the status quo of a large state—in this case the United States—that can act to balance the power of the Chinese state.

This framework of bigger-is-always-better stems from decades-old methods that remain popular among scholars and pundits who write on international relations and foreign policy.

The theory goes like this: regimes in states with economies with a large gross domestic product (GDP) have more access to resources. This means more access to weapons, food, personnel, and a variety of other resources necessary to carry out military operations or project power in the international sphere.

Consequently, theorists in international relations have long used the GDP (gross domestic product) and similar measures—such as the Composite Index of National Capability—as proxy measures for a state's power.[1]

The widespread use of these methods has led many to compare nations' foreign policy prowess based on aggregate measures. Nowadays, for example, it is common to hear how China, which has a GDP approaching that of the United States—is now a peer nation in terms of foreign policy and war-making power.

But this can be misleading. Aggregate measures are less useful than many imagine.

Certainly, GDP obviously has *something* to do with a state's ability to project power. It is, after all, a measure of production, and societies that can produce a large quantity of goods and services can presumably produce a large amount of weaponry while supplying large armies.

But measuring military capability isn't really this straightforward. Aggregate wealth measures like GDP cannot account for differences in the *net* wealth that a society enjoys. It is net wealth that really demonstrates a nation's power when it comes to international relations. Once we take these differences into account, we soon find that many large middle-income countries assumed to be very militarily powerful—a current example being China, of course—are not as powerful as assumed.

The Importance of Net Wealth and "Disposable Surplus"

Regimes in states with large populations usually have access to large amounts of resources. China and India, for example, are both among the top ten nations in terms of GDP. At first glance we might conclude that, in military terms, these states can therefore easily compare favorably against states with smaller economies and smaller aggregate GDPs. But there's much more to the equation than that. In many cases, a country's large output is due largely to its sizable population and not its economic efficiency or productivity. In a 2018 article in *International Security*, political scientist Michael

---

[1]For more on the Composite Indicator of National Capability, see The Correlates of War Project, https://correlatesofwar.org/data-sets/national-material-capabilities.

Beckley explained why a big population isn't always an asset for a state that desires to increase its power in the international sphere:

A big population is obviously an important power asset. Luxembourg, for example, will never be a great power, because its workforce is a blip in world markets and its army is smaller than Cleveland's police department. A big population, however, is no guarantee of great power status, because people both produce and consume resources; 1 billion peasants will produce immense output, but they also will consume most of that output on the spot, leaving few resources left over to buy global influence or build a powerful military.

To rank among the most powerful nations in the world, a state needs to amass a large stock of resources, and to do that a state must be big and efficient. It must produce high output at low costs. It must not only mobilize vast inputs, but also produce significant output per unit of input. In short, a nation's power stems not from its gross resources, but from its net resources—the resources left over after subtracting costs.[2]

The relative scarcity of net resources limits a state's ability to extract resources from the population for military purposes. While a state can theoretically starve a population—up to a point—in pursuit of military goals, this also presents significant political problems in terms of internal political resistance. Moreover, a starving population—or even an impoverished one—is not known for its efficiency in producing well-trained troops and high-quality military hardware.

Along these lines, Klaus Knorr, in his book *The War Potential of Nations*, points out that a state's control over some factors necessary for war making is decidedly limited. Variables like "minimum civilian consumption," "output of productive reserves," and "labor productivity" cannot be changed much via government fiat.[3] These are

---

[2]Michael Beckley, "The Power of Nations: Measuring What Matters," *International Security* 43, no. 2 (Fall 2018): 14, https://doi.org/10.1162/ISEC_a_00328. Klaus Knorr, *The War Potential of Nations* (Princeton, N.J.: Princeton University Press, 1956), pp. 231–32.

[3]Klaus Knorr, *The War Potential of Nations* (Princeton, N.J.: Princeton University Press, 1956), pp. 231–32.

limitations on state power. For Knorr, what matters is a state's "disposable surplus," or the amount of resources above and beyond what is necessary to maintain a politically acceptable standard of living for the bulk of the population.

We can see that a state from a nation with a relatively wealthy population, highly productive workers, and a standard of living far above subsistence is less limiting for state policy than a relatively unproductive workforce that lives closer to a subsistence level.

Nonetheless, international relations scholars have for decades focused primarily on aggregate resource totals. This has led to a reliance on GDP and the Composite Index of National Capability (CINC), which combines data on population, urban population, troop totals, military spending, iron and steel production, and energy consumption.

Why Do Smaller States Beat Larger States?

Beckley provides several examples of how these aggregate measures have failed to explain why smaller, richer countries often outperform much larger countries in international conflicts.

For example, why did China repeatedly lose to Britain in the Opium Wars during the nineteenth century? China had a much larger GDP than Britain at this time, and indeed, Britain never overtook China in terms of GDP. Although the CINC measure suggests a British advantage for the period, the advantage was by no means overwhelming. Yet Britain repeatedly devastated China in a series of military conflicts.

Nor can aggregate measures explain why Japan repeatedly humiliated China during the late nineteenth and early twentieth centuries. During this period—as today—China's GDP was far larger than Japan's. The CINC measure for the period shows an even bigger advantage for China against Japan. But Japan repeatedly prevailed.

Aggregate measures also fail to explain how Germany handily defeated Russia on the eastern front during the First World War. On paper, in terms of GDP, Germany and Russia were nearly evenly matched. According to the CINC measure, Russia held the advantage. But Germany overwhelmed the Russian Empire during the war, and the Russian regime collapsed soon after.

To see the questionable explanatory power of aggregate measures in a "cold war," we need look no further than the conflict between the Soviet Union and the United States. Although the US held an advantage in GDP in the 1970s and 1980s, the CINC for that period indicates a Soviet advantage. By the 1970s, the Soviet Union was the world leader in terms of army size and military research and development. Moreover, "the chief analyst of the Soviet Union in the US Central Intelligence Agency...concluded that the Soviet Union was twice as powerful as the United States, and rising."[4]

Although the Soviet Union had a larger population than the US and was *three times* the physical size of the US, the Soviet Union essentially surrendered to the US in the Cold War in 1990.

In these cases we find that countries with smaller economies and smaller populations are often, in fact, the more powerful states in interstate conflicts. It is the more productive, well-organized, and wealthier nations that hold the advantage. The CINC measure distorts reality in modern times as well. As Beckley notes, if we used the CINC as a gauge of global power, we would conclude that:

> Israel is, and has always been, one of the weakest countries in the Middle East; Singapore is one of the weakest in Southeast Asia; Brazil dominates South America with roughly five times the power resources of any other state; Russia dominated Europe throughout the 1990s, with more power resources than Germany, France, and the United Kingdom combined; and China has dominated the world since 1996 and currently has twice the power resources of the United States.[5]

Obviously, none of these scenarios are true in real life.

Measuring Foreign Policy Power More Accurately

Much of the problem in describing relative power in these cases stems from the fact that GDP and CINC exaggerate population as

---

[4]Beckley, "The Power of Nations," p. 33.
[5]Ibid., p. 41.

an advantage. Rather, it would be better to come up with a formula that takes a more realistic view of the relative importance of both wealth and population size. But how can we measure this?

In this, Beckley takes a cue from Swiss economic historian Paul Bairoch, who suggested that the "strength of a nation could be found in a formula combining per capita and total GDP."[6]

Why use GDP per capita? The reason for this can be found in the fact that GDP per capita is a fairly reliable proxy for economic development. More developed nations are better at many things that make a state more likely to win in military power and power projection. Developed economies have more efficient workers, more reliable technology, more durable materials, more technically skilled soldiers, etc. More developed countries are also able to produce large amounts of weaponry without devastating drops in the population's standard of living. In other words, highly developed societies are more efficient.

So, it's not enough to look to measures that are heavily influenced by total population size. Beckley explains how incorporating GDP per capita into measures of power is important in putting total population size into proper perspective:

> Dividing GDP by population controls for some of the costs that make the difference between a state's gross and net resources. Combining GDP with GDP per capita thus yields an indicator that accounts for size and efficiency, the two main dimensions of net resources.
>
> To create a rough proxy for net resources, I follow Bairoch's advice by simply multiplying GDP by GDP per capita, creating an index that gives equal weight to a nation's gross output and its output per person. This two-variable index obviously does not measure net resources directly, nor does it resolve all of the shortcomings of GDP and CINC. By penalizing population, however, it provides a better sense of a nation's net resources than GDP, CINC, or other gross indicators alone.[7]

---

[6]Paul Bairoch, "Europe's Gross National Product: 1800–1975," *Journal of European Economic History* 5, no. 2 (Fall 1976): 282.

[7]Beckley, "The Power of Nations, p. 19.

With this method, it becomes more clear why comparatively smaller, less populous, less militarized countries (i.e., Britain in the nineteenth century) have so often prevailed against states that rule over larger economies and larger populations.

This is, of course, relevant to modern comparisons between China and the United States. If we look at 2020's nominal GDP totals, we find that China's GDP is approaching that of the United States. China's GDP is 70 percent the size of the US's GDP, and the second largest in the world. The US comes in at $20 trillion while China's GDP is $14 trillion.[8]

This would seem to make China a fairly even match for the United States, especially when fighting on its own turf. Moreover, the CINC measure, using the most recent index data—for 2007— shows China has an *advantage*. According to the Correlates of War Project, China's CINC index value is 0.19, but the US's value is only 0.14.[9]

But what about GDP per capita? According to the International Monetary Fund, per capita GDP in the United States in 2020 was $63,051. In China, per capita GDP was $17,206. That's only 27 percent the size of the US measure.

If we use Beckley's formula and "simply multipl[y] GDP by GDP per capita," we find that China's advantage disappears. By this measure, the US's power is more than three times that of China.[10] Although much is made of the US regime's debt and the declining relative power, the fact is China suffers from all the same economic ailments the US does but without the high levels of worker productivity and without America's dozens of economic allies worldwide.

---

[8]If we consider purchasing power parity, China GDP is slightly larger than that of the US.

[9]The Correlates of War Project.

[10]This incorporates purchasing power parity into GDP and GDP per capita comparisons. If nominal values are used, the US is five times as powerful as China under the GDPxGDP per capita calculation.

What If the Red States and Blue States Split Up?

This debate over whether or not "bigger is better" has much relevance to the debate over secession in the United States. China certainly isn't the only country that matters as far as American international relations are concerned. But it is likely to be held up as the great bogeyman and the reason for why secessionists must never be allowed to succeed. So, even if we illustrate—as we do above—that the United States in its current form holds a sizable advantage over a more resource-starved China, how would things look if the US were to break up into smaller pieces?

We could play out many different scenarios, of course, but just as one of many potential thought experiments, let's assume the United States devolves into only two new countries: the Blue States of America (BSA) and the Red States of America (RSA).

These two new countries are composed of the following states:

Red (27 states): Alabama, Alaska, Arizona, Arkansas, Florida, Georgia, Idaho, Indiana, Iowa, Kansas, Kentucky, Louisiana, Mississippi, Missouri, Montana, Nebraska, Ohio, Oklahoma, North Carolina, North Dakota, South Carolina, South Dakota, Tennessee, Texas, Utah, West Virginia, and Wyoming.

Blue (23 states, plus DC): California, Colorado, Connecticut, Delaware, District of Columbia, Hawaii, Illinois, Maine, Maryland, Massachusetts, Michigan, Minnesota, Nevada, New Hampshire, New Jersey, New Mexico, New York, Oregon, Pennsylvania, Rhode Island, Vermont, Virginia, Washington, Wisconsin.

As American leftists are often happy to point out, blue America—at least in the aggregate—is richer than red America. This is largely due to the presence of a large number of big, productive cities in the blue states. As a result, the BSA (Blue-State America) contains most of the USA's current $21 trillion GDP: $12.3 trillion. The BSA contains 170 million residents, for an overall per capita GDP of $73,000.

In the RSA (Red-State America), these numbers are smaller. In the 27 states, total GDP is $8.9 trillion, spread out over a population of 158 million. The GDP per capita is $56,000.

In terms of economic power, both of these new countries remain near the top of the heap. The BSA, of course, has a per capita GDP among the highest in the world, right behind Ireland, and ahead of Switzerland. The total GDP for the BSA is behind only the EU and China, and larger than those of India, Japan, and Germany.

In the RSA, the per capita GDP puts it well within the company of wealthy nations. At $56,000, it's right between Austria and the Netherlands. Total GDP, although behind that of the BSA, is about equal to India's, and remains larger than those of Japan, Germany, and all the rest.

Using the Beckley-Bairoch approach, we find that the relative military power in both the BSA and the RSA is *still* larger than that of the Chinese regime. Naturally, neither has the total military resources of the United States as a whole, but great wealth goes a long way in either case.

This is just a very basic calculation, but it's easy to see how successor states to the US would retain advantages over China even if the US broke up into several smaller pieces. China would still have all the usual troubles in its own backyard. No matter how many new pieces the United States might devolve into, the fact remains that North America is insulated from Asia and Europe by two oceans. In China, meanwhile, the regime:

> does not devote all, and perhaps not even a majority, of its military resources to contingencies involving the United States. China shares sea or land borders with nineteen countries, five of which fought wars against China within the last century; its northern and western borders are porous and populated by disaffected minority groups; and its government faces a constant threat of domestic rebellion. As a result, the People's Liberation Army (PLA) devotes substantial resources to internal security and requires 300,000 troops just to police China's borders....In a separate study, I found that developing countries systematically fail at warfare, regardless of the size of their defense budgets, because they lack the economic capacity to maintain, modernize, and integrate individual technologies into cohesive military systems.[11]

---

[11]Michael Beckley, "China's Century?" *International Security* 36, no. 3 (Winter 2011/12): 41–78.

Sovereign States, but Allies Too

We've been assuming so far, however, that these post secession states in North America would have to each face China independently in case of a clash. This, however, is not a good assumption. It is not at all a given that these independent states would shun the idea of mutual defense. In fact, experience suggests the opposite. This is apparent even to those who are not exactly entrenched advocates for secession. As noted by Eric Sammons at the conservative *Crisis Magazine*:

> Foreign policy presents another challenge for an American secession movement. Secession opponents fear weakening American hegemony across the world. Would a divided America result in greater global influence for China or Russia? Would it lead to a possible invasion by those countries?
>
> It's impossible to say for sure, but there is no reason that a divided America could not remain a confederation of allies when it comes to military defense. An attack on any one new American nation-state could be considered an attack on all nation-states.[12]

This observation that a NATO-like institution for North America could easily arise should be obvious to anyone who's noticed that countries with similar backgrounds—think Canada, the USA, Australia, and the UK—have been generally united on foreign policy for over a century now.

In spite of this, it's not uncommon to hear claims that neighboring states are all poised to go to war with each other at any given moment. This, we are told, would be the natural outcome if the United States allows any portion of the nation to become independent. These anti-secessionists often point to examples like the Yugoslav wars and claim ethnic cleansing is on the horizon. But North America isn't southeastern Europe. In the case of North America, we'd be dealing with countries that share a common language, a

---

[12]Eric Sammons, "The Catholic Case for Secession?" *Crisis Magazine*, December 23, 2020, https://www.crisismagazine.com/2020/the-catholic-case-for-secession.

high standard of living—and thus much to lose from an internecine war—and have deep and extensive trade relations.

Moreover, if one is going to claim that two nations with such similar backgrounds are bound to go to war, one will need to explain why Canada has been at peace with the United States for 206 years. Conceivably, one might claim this is only because Canada was too small to challenge the US. But this ignores the fact that Canadian foreign policy was set by Britain—a world power and peer of the US—until 1931.[13] Yet, in all those years after the War of 1812, during which the British state shared both extensive land and maritime borders with the US through British Canadian domains, London was apparently uninterested in war with the US.

However, we're expected to believe that if the United States were to break into smaller independent states, the "Blue States of America" will welcome a Chinese invasion of, say, Tampa Bay just to stick it to the red states. This may seem plausible to more paranoid anti-China Cold Warriors who seem to believe every left-of-center American is an agent of Beijing. But the Tampa Bay scenario is about as likely as Canada asking the People's Liberation Army to invade Boston.

Conclusion

The importance of looking beyond aggregate measures of military power naturally extends beyond the relationship between the US and China. We find similar situations when we use the Beckley method to look at European states' power relative to Russia. Russia's GDP per capita, for example, is only about half that of Germany, and when we compare the two states by combining GDP and GDP per capita, Germany's military efficiency is five times that of Russia. Combining Germany's potential military power with that of other European states, like France or the UK, Russia remains far, far behind its supposed western European adversaries.

Obviously, no single measure can provide a complete picture of the many factors relevant to analyzing the relative power of states.

---

[13]The British Parliament passed the Statute of Westminster in 1931, effectively granting *de jure* sovereignty to Canada.

Yet pundits and scholars who comment on international relations have for too long relied on crude aggregate measures which suggest far higher levels of relative military power than is likely in cases like Russia and China, or even India, Brazil, and many Arab states. This isn't to say that states like China or Russia are irrelevant. Their sizable conventional militaries mean they can indeed project power onto their immediate neighbors, just as the US can. But it is not the case that large, populous states hold all the cards. Economic development—which, we know, tends to be more developed in smaller and more decentralized states—is likely a more critical factor.

13

If America Splits Up, What Happens to the Nukes?

Opposition to American secession movements often hinges on the idea that foreign policy concerns trump any notions that the United States ought to be broken up into smaller pieces. It almost goes without saying that those who subscribe to neoconservative ideology, or views favoring interventionist foreign policy, treat the idea of political division with alarm or contempt. Or both.

These activists fear that if the US were broken up into smaller pieces, it would be weakened in its ability to act as a global hegemon. This would threaten the US's current foreign-policy toolkit: invading foreign nations at will, imposing "regime change," and threatening war with any regime that opposes the whims of the American regime.

For some of us, however, this would be a *feature* of secession rather than a bug.

Moreover, the ability of the American regime to carry out offensive military operations such as regime change is separate and distinct from the regime's ability to maintain an effective and credible *defensive* military force.

Even a dismembered United States would be more than capable of fielding a large and effective defensive military force. A politically divided America remains a very wealthy America, and wealth remains a key component in effective military defense.[1] Indeed, as we've seen in previous chapters, a group of smaller, decentralized American states is likely to *benefit* economically from decentralization, further enhancing military capabilities. In other words, bigness is not as important as the extent to which a regime can call upon high levels of wealth and capital accumulation. That analysis, however, concentrated on conventional forces and this leaves us with the question of how the successor states to a post-secession United States would fare in terms of nuclear deterrence. In this case, there is even less need for bigness than in the case of conventional military forces. As the state of Israel has demonstrated, a small state can obtain the benefits of nuclear deterrence without a large population or a large economy. An effective military defense through nuclear deterrence is even more economical than conventional military forces.

Is Proliferation Good?

Before we can proceed, we must address the issue of nuclear proliferation. Since the Second World War, the dominant position in the US military establishment has been that the US regime must be willing to expend enormous amounts of resources to prevent nuclear proliferation—while simultaneously maintaining an enormous nuclear arsenal at the disposal of the US itself. It is assumed that proliferation beyond a small number of states is likely to lead to instability and catastrophic results. The costs and side effects of pursuing a global non-proliferation regime, on the other hand, are not often addressed.

The first influential theories to express doubts about the established non-proliferation narrative was Kenneth Waltz. As summarized by Henry Sokolski:

---

[1] Robert O. Keohane, *After Hegemony: Cooperation and Discord in the World Political Economy* (Princeton, N.J.: Princeton University Press. 1984), pp. 22–25.

In 1981, Kenneth Waltz popularized French and American finite deterrence thinking of the late-1950s by asking whether or not nuclear weapons in more hands might be better. His answer was yes. As nuclear weapons spread, he argued, adversaries would view war as being self-defeating, and peace would become more certain.[2]

Or, as George Perkovich put it, Waltz "has been the most illustrious proponent" of the view that "The one major benefit of nuclear proliferation conceivably would be to create deterrence relationships that lower or eliminate the risk of war between a certain set of adversaries."[3]

Waltz was not alone. In more recent decades, Harvey Sapolsky has concluded that nuclear nonproliferation can expand the risk of nuclear war by extending US nuclear guarantees over a rising number of states. By extending nuclear guarantees as a means of preventing proliferation, the nonproliferation regime has the potential to turn regional conflicts—which may sometimes tragically turn regional nuclear conflicts into global ones:

> I fear…we have more to fear as a nation from the costs of extended deterrence than form the need to deter additional nuclear-armed enemies…[4]

Moreover, Sapolsky notes the nonproliferation effort has not actually stopped proliferation, with India, Israel, Pakistan, and North Korea all having become nuclear-armed states since the implementation of the Nonproliferation Treaty (NPT) in 1970. The fact these new nuclear states have not engaged in nuclear war

---

[2]Henry D. Sokolski, "Introduction: Is Nuclear Proliferation Still a Problem?," in *Should We Let the Bomb Spread*, ed. Henry D. Sokolski (Carlisle Barracks, Penn.: United States Army War College Press, 2016), p. xiii.

[3]George Perkovich, "Could Anything Be Done to Stop Them? Lessons from Pakistan's Proliferating Past," in *Pakistan's Nuclear Future: Worries Beyond War*, ed. Henry D. Sokolski (Carlisle, Penn.: Strategic Studies Institute, 2008), p. 78.

[4]Harvey M. Sapolsky, "Getting Past Nonproliferation," in *Should We Let the Bomb Spread*, ed. Henry D. Sokolski (Carlisle Barracks, Penn.: United States Army War College Press, 2016), p. 1.

cannot be attributed to the existence of a nonproliferation treaty, but to the realities of nuclear deterrence as described by Waltz— and by Bertrand Lemennicier in his game-theory based analysis "Nuclear Weapons: Proliferation or Monopoly?"[5]

The benefits of deterrence also factor in to John Mearsheimers's writings in favor of limited proliferation, most notably in the context of Mearsheimer's conclusion that Ukraine would have benefited from maintaining its own nuclear arsenal in the wake of the collapse of the Soviet Union.[6]

Sapolsky concludes that, for a variety of reasons, "not many nations will seek to acquire nuclear weapons," even in the absence of a nonproliferation regime.[7] He goes on to note, rather, that "[t]he biggest obstacle to getting beyond the NPT is the fear of terrorists using a stolen or otherwise nefariously obtained nuclear weapon to blackmail or destroy civilization."[8]

On this, John Mueller has written numerous books and articles.[9] Mueller has explained that states—even rogue ones—have no motivation to transfer the control of nuclear weapons to those outside the state's control. One problem a rogue dictator or oligarch faces is that "there would be too much risk—even for a country led by extremists—that the ultimate source of the weapon would be discovered." Mueller notes an even greater danger:

> [T]here is a very considerable danger to the donor that the bomb (and its source) would be discovered before delivery, or that it would be exploded in a manner and on a target the donor would not approve of—including on the donor itself. Another concern

---

[5]Bertrand Lemennicier, "Nuclear Weapons: Proliferation or Monopoly?," in *The Myth of National Defense,* ed. Hans-Hermann Hoppe (Auburn, Ala.: Mises Institute, 2003), pp. 127–43.

[6]John J. Mearsheimer, "The Case for a Ukrainian Nuclear Deterrent," *Foreign Affairs* 72, no. 3 (Summer 1993): 52.

[7]Sapolsky, p. 13

[8]Ibid., p. 15.

[9]See John Mueller, *Atomic Obsession: Nuclear Alarmism from Hiroshima to al-Qaeda* (New York: Oxford University Press, 2010.)

would be that the terrorist group might be infiltrated by foreign intelligence.[10]

And finally, there are no known cases of "loose nukes," even in the wake of the collapse of the Soviet Union:

> A careful assessment conducted by the Center for Nonproliferation Studies has concluded that it is unlikely that any of those devices have been lost and that, regardless, their effectiveness would be very low or even nonexistent because they (like all nuclear weapons) require continual maintenance. Even some of those people most alarmed by the prospect of atomic terrorism have concluded, "It is probably true that there are no 'loose nukes,' transportable nuclear weapons missing from their proper storage locations and available for purchase in some way."[11]

I do not seek to reconstruct or add to the arguments already made by scholars who have already challenged the common position that proliferation is always and everywhere too dangerous to tolerate. Waltz, Sapolsky, Mueller, and others have provided a useful foundation on which to consider the matter. Ultimately, however, any discussion of secession and the deconstruction of large states into smaller states must address the issue of proliferation because post-secession successor states will have to deal with the maintenance, transfer, or seizure of such weapons when secessionists are able to assert and maintain sovereignty within a new state. An excessive emphasis on nonproliferation tends to produce a bias overwhelmingly in favor of the status quo and stability for existing states—including very large states. This, of course, is a significant obstacle to support for radical decentralization.

After Secession, Who Gets the Nukes?

To gain a better understanding of these issues, we can look to the past to see how secession can actually play out when nuclear weapons are involved. One example we might consider is Ukraine's

---

[10]John Mueller, "'At all Costs': The Destructive Consequences of Anti-Proliferation Policy," in *Should We Let the Bomb Spread*, ed. Henry D. Sokolski (Carlisle Barracks, Penn.: United States Army War College Press, 2016), p. 76.

[11]Ibid., p. 77.

secession from the Soviet Union in the early 1990s. In 1991, as the Soviet Union was collapsing, Ukrainians voted overwhelmingly to secede and set up an independent republic. At the time, the new state of Ukraine contained around one-third of the Soviet nuclear arsenal. This means there were literally thousands of nuclear warheads within Ukraine's borders, making Ukraine's arsenal the third largest in the world. In 1994, Ukraine began a program of denuclearization and today is no longer a nuclear power.

The relations between Ukraine and the new Russian Federation were acrimonious in the early nineties—as now—so this means that the lessons of the Ukraine situation are limited if applied to American secessionist movements. American pundits may like to play up the red-blue division in America as an intractable conflict of civilizations, but these differences are small potatoes compared to the sort of ethnic and nationalist conflicts that have long existed in Eurasia. Nevertheless, we can glean some insights from that separation.

For example, the Ukrainian secession demonstrates that it is possible for nuclear weapons to pass into the control of a seceding state without a general conflict breaking out. Indeed, Ukraine was not alone in this. Kazakhstan and Belarus "inherited" nuclear arms from the Soviet Union as well. If Russia, Ukraine, Kazakhstan, and Belarus can all peacefully negotiate a resolution on how to deal with a suddenly decentralized nuclear arsenal, the Americans can pull it off, too.

Nonetheless, the Ukraine situation highlights some of the technical and logistical problems involved in working out who exactly controls nuclear weapons in a post-secession situation.

For example, it was never a simple matter for the Ukrainian regime to assert technical control over land-based nuclear missiles. It is unlikely that Ukraine ever obtained all the tools necessary to actually launch the nuclear missiles within its territory.[12]

It *is* likely, however, that Ukraine could have *eventually* gained this power, as it was already developing its own control system for the arsenal in 1993. Not surprisingly, the Russian regime was

---

[12]John J. Mearsheimer, "The Case for a Ukrainian Nuclear Deterrent," *Foreign Affairs* 72, no. 3 (Summer 1993): 52.

unenthusiastic about helping the Ukrainians in this respect. When it came to using nuclear-capable bombers, on the other hand, it appears Ukraine's regime had total control.[13]

It is likely the successor states of the US would face similar issues. The use of land-based missiles would be heavily reliant on authorization from whichever faction most recently controlled access and launching authority, even if those missiles are physically located within the borders of a separatist state. It must be noted, however, that the state within which land-based nuclear missiles exist has the ability to prevent usage in most cases. This is because even if the missiles themselves cannot be directly controlled, the personnel that maintains and controls the sites can far more easily be traded out for personnel loyal to the new regime.[14]

When it comes to submarines and bombers, a secessionist US region might find itself better able to assert control in the short term. Where those bombers and subs end up would have a lot to do with the likely chaotic situation in the wake of the independence movement and shifting borders.

Separatist Regions May Be Unwilling to Give Up Nukes

Ukraine had denuclearized in part due to bribes and pressure from both the United States and Russia.[15] Russia wanted Ukraine's

---

[13]Ibid., p. 52.

[14]"Good News From Ukraine: It Doesn't Have Nukes," *National Interest*, March 21, 2014, https://www.belfercenter.org/publication/good-news-ukraine-it-doesnt-have-nukes. Graham Allison notes the importance of personnel in the post-Soviet Ukraine situation in the *National Interest*: "Officially, the chain-of-command continued to run from the new President of Russia through communications and control systems to missile officers in Ukraine. Physically, however, the missiles, warheads, officers, and mechanisms for launching weapons resided on the territory of Ukraine. Moreover, the individuals who operated these systems now lived in houses owned by the government of Ukraine, received paychecks from the Ministry of Defense of Ukraine, and were subject to promotion or firing not by Moscow, but by Kiev."

[15]Ted Galen Carpenter, "Ukraine's Surrender of Its Nukes Was a Major Strategic Blunder," *National Interest*, September 24, 2019, https://nationalinterest.org/blog/buzz/ukraines-surrender-its-nukes-was-major-strategic-blunder-83026.

arsenal for obvious reasons. The United States was obsessed with deproliferation, although it naturally insisted on keeping its *own* massive stockpile.

Neither the US nor Russia had the ability to *force* Ukraine to denuclearize—short of a full-scale invasion of Ukraine, of course. However, Ukraine capitulated to pressure when the Russian Federation, the US, and the UK (and to a lesser extent China and France) pledged in the Budapest Memorandum to protect Ukraine's territorial integrity.

In 2014, many interpreted this move as a grand folly when Russia annexed the Crimea from Ukraine and none of the other parties to the memorandum intervened. Ukraine had given up its best guarantee against Russian intervention—its nuclear arsenal—in exchange for weak "assurances" from foreign states.

Some foreign policy scholars—most notably Mearsheimer—had predicted this and advised against denuclearization in Ukraine. Indeed, in 1993, Mearsheimer doubted that Ukraine would cave to denuclearization pressure precisely because reliable assurances from outsiders were unlikely. Even after the Budapest Memorandum became a reality a year later, it was nonetheless a rather weak reed on which to hang denuclearization. As Mearsheimer pointed out, should the Americans fail to provide an effective defense for Ukraine—as ended up being the case with the Crimea crisis—the Americans "would not have to live with the consequences of a Russian attack."[16] Nonetheless, some Ukrainians insist the Crimea crisis is not evidence of a need for a nuclear deterrent.[17]

Many Americans, however, may be much less sanguine—even to the point of unwarranted paranoia—about the prospects of foreign intervention on American soil. This is why it is best to proceed assuming that at least some successor states to the current US would insist on retaining a nuclear arsenal. After all, while Ukraine might

---

[16]Ibid., p. 58.

[17]"Ukraine has no ambitions to becomenuclear power again—Poroshenko," *Interfax-Ukraine*, Ukraine News Agency, December 12, 2014, https://en.interfax.com.ua/news/economic/239730.html.

have been betting on the US as the enforcer of the international order, such guarantees would be even more unlikely in the wake of an American secession crisis. Some post-secession American states may seek a self-help system of deterrence.

On the other hand, we should not assume that *all* successor states to the United States would seek permanent nuclear arsenals. Some would likely give up nuclear programs, just as Sweden and South Africa have abandoned nuclear programs that were nearing completion. While the Ukrainian example of voluntary denuclearization may appear to be a blunder to many now, the situation in North America is different. North America is not eastern Europe with its long history of interstate conflict. In North America, Canada and the United States have been at peace for more than two centuries, and Canada has never made much effort to move toward assembling a nuclear arsenal. Rather, Canada's proximity to the United States *shields* it from nuclear threats from outside North America. Any conventional or nuclear arrack on Canada from, say, China or Russia is likely to be interpreted as an attack on the United States, with disastrous consequences for the initial aggressor.

In other words, Canada benefits from what Baldur Thorhallsson calls "shelter" in the international arena.[18] Canada requires no nuclear arsenal of its own, because it can use its close alliance with the United States as a substitute.

So long as *some* successor states of the United States maintain a functioning arsenal, other nonnuclear states in North America will be able to function similarly. It stands to reason that just as the United States in its current form has been at peace with all other former British colonies, it is likely that new North American republics will share a similar fate.

---

[18]Baldur Thorhallsson, "A small state in world politics: Iceland's search for shelter," *Icelandic Review of Politics and Administration*, May 31, 2018, http://www.irpa.is/article/view/a.2018.14.1.3.

Big States Are Not Necessary: A Deterrent Nuclear Force Is Entirely Feasible for Small States

A new American republic need not be especially large to maintain a working arsenal.

While a sizable economy and population are extremely helpful in terms of building a large conventional military, these factors are not nearly as important when it comes to a nuclear force capable of deterring foreign powers.

As Waltz has explained, "Nuclear parity is reached when countries have second-strike forces. It does not require quantitative or qualitative equality of forces."[19] If a regime can plausibly hide or move around enough nuclear warheads—"enough" being well under one hundred warheads—to survive a nuclear first strike, that regime is able to deter nuclear aggression from other states altogether.[20]

This is why Waltz has concluded that "deterrence is easier to contrive than most strategists have believed"[21] and that "some countries may find nuclear weapons a cheaper and safer alternative to running economically ruinous and militarily dangerous conventional arms races. Nuclear weapons may promise increased security and independence at an affordable price."[22] In other words, deterrence "can be implemented cheaply."[23]

The Israeli state is an important and illustrative case. This is a country with a GDP smaller than Colorado's and a population smaller than that of the US state of Georgia. Yet, Israel is thought

---

[19]Kenneth Waltz, "Structural Realism after the Cold War," *International Security* 25, no. 1 (Summer 2000): 5–41, esp. 32–75.

[20]Kenneth Waltz, "Nuclear Myths and Political Realities," *American Political Science Review* 84, no. 3 (September 1990): 731–45.

[21]Ibid.

[22]Kenneth Waltz, "The Spread of Nuclear Weapons: More May Be Better," *Adelphi Papers* 21, no. 171 (1981).

[23]Kenneth N. Waltz, "Nuclear Myths and Political Realities," in *The Use of Force: Military Power and International Politics*, eds. Robert J. Art, Kenneth N. Waltz (Oxford, U.K.: Rowman and Littlefield, 2004), p. 113.

to maintain a nuclear triad of sea, air, and land-based warheads. This is a small state which has taken full advantage of the relatively economical nature of a small nuclear arsenal (estimated to include approximately eighty assembled warheads).

The Value of Minimum Deterrence

Whether or not politicians believe in the use of minimum deterrence has little to do with whether or not it is actually effective, and arms agreements like New START don't do much to push regimes in this direction.

In a 1990 essay titled "Nuclear Myths and Political Realities," Waltz outlines how "strategic arms agreements do not have military, but economic and political, significance."[24]

Counting up the total number of missiles in these enormous arsenals does little, since, for nations that are already well above the threshold of achieving nuclear deterrence, these treaties don't change the military calculus.

What really matters is the perception that the other side has second-strike capability, and this certainly exists in US-Russia relations. Once each regime knows that the other regime has second-strike capability, the competition is over. Deterrence is established. Waltz notes:

> So long as two or more countries have second-strike forces, to compare them is pointless. If no state can launch a disarming attack with high confidence, force comparisons become irrelevant....Within very wide ranges, a nuclear balance is insensitive to variation in numbers and size of warheads.[25]

The focus on second-strike capability is key because pro-arms-race policymakers are quick to note that if a regime is able (with a first strike) to destroy its enemy's ability to retaliate in kind, then a nuclear war can be "won."

---

[24]Ibid., p. 107.
[25]Ibid., p. 103.

Second-Strike Capability Evens the Score

But, as shown by Michael Gerson in *International Security* (2010) establishing second-strike capability—or, more importantly, the *perception* that a regime has it—is not as difficult as many suppose. Gerson writes:

> A successful first strike would require near-perfect intelligence, surveillance, and reconnaissance (ISR) to detect, identify, and track all of the adversary's nuclear forces; recent events surrounding U.S. assessments of Iraq's suspected WMD [weapons of mass destruction] capabilities forcefully demonstrate the challenges of reliable, accurate, and unbiased information. Intelligence regarding where an adversary's nuclear weapons are located and if the state is actually planning to attack could be wrong or incomplete, and an attempted first strike based on inaccurate or incomplete information could have far-reaching negative consequences.[26]

This can be countered through a variety of methods, including secrecy and the ability to move weapons delivery systems around. This is why the US, Russian, and Chinese regimes have long been so enthusiastic about the so-called nuclear triad. It is assumed that if nuclear weapons can be delivered by submarine, aircraft, and land, then it would be impossible for an opposing regime to destroy all three at once and achieve first-strike victory.

But even in the absence of a triad, an opposing regime that seeks a total first-strike victory has few grounds for much confidence. As Waltz shows, "Nuclear weapons are small and light; they are easy to move, easy to hide, and easy to deliver in a variety of ways." That is, if a regime manages to move around and hide even a small number of planes, subs, or trucks, this could spell disaster for the regime attempting a successful first strike. Gerson explains:

> A nuclear first strike is fraught with risk and uncertainty. Could a US president, the only person with the power to authorize nuclear use and a political official concerned with re-election, his or her political party, and their historical legacy, ever be entirely confident

---

[26]Michael S. Gerson, "No First Use," *International Security* 35, no. 2 (Fall 2010): 26.

that the mission would be a complete success? What if the strike failed to destroy all of the weapons, or what if weapons were hidden in unknown areas, and the remaining weapons were used in retaliation?[27]

Nor must it be assumed that a *large* number of warheads is necessary to achieve deterrence. Waltz recalls that Desmond Ball—who had advised the US on escalation strategies[28]—convincingly asserted that the nuclear weapons necessary for deterrence numbered "not in the hundreds but in the tens."[29] Ball contended that a debilitating attack on the US could be achieved with as few as fifty warheads.[30]

Proceeding on the assumption that an enemy has no warheads left following a first strike requires an extremely high level of confidence, because the cost of miscalculation is so high. If a regime initiates a first strike and misses only a few of the enemy's missiles, this could lead to devastating retaliation both in terms of human life and in terms of the first-strike regime's political prospects.

This is why Waltz concludes that a rudimentary nuclear force can achieve deterrence if there is even a small and plausible chance of second-strike capability. A small nuclear strike is nonetheless disastrous for the target, and thus "second-strike forces have to be seen in absolute terms." Waltz correctly insists that calculating the relative dominance of one arsenal over another becomes a waste of time: "the question of dominance is pointless because one second-strike force cannot dominate another."[31]

The conclusion is that a small second-strike force is sufficient. Naturally, this can be attractive to smaller or cash-strapped regimes, such as the Soviet Union, which in its final decades found itself devoting ever larger amounts of its GDP to military spending.

---

[27]Ibid.

[28]David Wroe, "Des Ball: the man who saved the world," *The Sydney Morning Herald*, December 21, 2012.

[29]Waltz, "Nuclear Myths and Political Realities," p. 105.

[30]Drew Middleton, "Study Says Nuclear War Can't Be Controlled," *The New York Times*, November 18, 1981.

[31]Waltz, "Nuclear Myths and Political Realities," p. 105.

A Minority View

This remains the minority view. Nikita Khrushchev, for example, faced much opposition to his plans to adopt a minimum deterrence posture in the Soviet Union after 1961. Conservatives in the military and Politburo were vehemently opposed to the plan, in part because it included cutting back on spending on conventional military forces. But the opposition was also due to the fact that the hardliners were quite convinced by the perceived necessity of immense, flexible, and overwhelming force.[32]

In the United States, of course, minimum deterrence has never been very popular, especially among conservatives. For example, spending on the US nuclear arsenal increased 50 percent under Donald Trump from 2016 to 2020. The Pentagon and Congress continue to put sizable faith in maintaining a large, diverse, and expensive arsenal.

In any case, the rejection of minimum deterrence achieves a useful political goal, as described by Waltz:

> The claim that we need a seamless web of capabilities in order to deter does serve one purpose: it keeps military budgets wondrously high.[33]

Clearly, claims that even medium-sized American states—such as Ohio with 11 million people and a GDP nearly as large as that of Switzerland—are too small to contemplate functioning as independent states are unconvincing. Moreover, there is no reason to assume any postsecession American state would seek to act alone in the realm of international relations. Kirkpatrick Sale has pointed out what should be regarded as obvious: "Historically, the response of small states to the threat of...aggression has been temporary confederation and mutual defense, and indeed *the simple threat of such unity*, in the form of defense treaties and leagues and alliances, has sometimes been a sufficient deterrent" (emphasis added).[34]

---

[32]John Erickson, "Détente, Deterrence, and Military Superiority: A Soviet Dilemma," *World Today* 21, no. 8 (August 1965): 339, 344.

[33]Waltz, "Nuclear Myths and Political Realities," p. 127.

[34]Kirkpatrick Sale, *Human Scale Revisited* (White River Junction, Vt.: Chelsea Green, 2017), p. 312.

On the other hand, a continuation of the current trend toward political centralization in Washington—and the growing political domination of every corner of the nation by central authorities—is likely to only harm future prospects for amicable separation and peaceful cooperation on the international stage.

Part II
Decentralization and Democracy

14

Why "One Man, One Vote" Doesn't Work

I t has increasingly become a central tenet of social-democratic thinking that all democratic systems must employ a "one man, one vote" framework. This, however, is just one more tool states use to undermine the benefits of political decentralization.

Rather, "one man, one vote" works to diminish the power of electoral groups within specific regions or populations of a polity. The effect is to politically homogenize a voting population, further crippling the ability of under-represented minority populations to combat the imagined "national will" of the majority. "One man, one vote" is not a clearly defined concept, but one central characteristic of this type of system is that it does not allow for schemes of representation employed in federal systems like those in Switzerland and the United States.

In the United States, for example, a central institution of federalism is the US Senate in which each member state is given an equal vote. This allows for relatively greater representation for regional interests that cannot hope to compete in terms of raw voting numbers within the national population overall.

The US is not alone in using such measures. The Australian Senate, for example, allots twelve members to each state. The Senate of Canada is composed of appointed members who represent regions rather than individual provinces. Regional representation of this sort is not based on population size as in the House of Commons. In the Swiss Council of States, each canton is represented by two members, regardless of size.[1]

Other non-majoritarian methods are used as well. The American electoral college system is one example. Another example is the Swiss method of "double majority," in which some legislation requires approval by both the overall Swiss population (using a "one man, one vote" principle) but also by a majority vote in a majority of the cantons.

The purpose here is to make it easier for national minorities to veto or impede legislation desired by the majority. In other words, democratic power is decentralized among numerous jurisdictions rather than in a single jurisdiction. Without this form of decentralization, a simple majority of the whole would be all that is necessary to maintain political control in a democratic state. This method of allotting political power becomes problematic, however, because it often renders minority interests essentially powerless.

For example, it might be the case that in the US House of Representatives—which employs a "one man, one vote" representation scheme—a small number of populous and urban states can easily pass legislation that is unfavorable to farmers. When political representation is based only on population, the outnumbered farmers cannot hope to defeat this legislation. In the US Senate, on the other hand, where all states receive equal representation, the relatively numerous

---

[1]Into the mid-twentieth century, individual US states often employed non-population-based apportionment in their own senates. In some cases, each county was represented by one or two senators, regardless of the county's size. Eventually in the federal courts, the "one man, one vote" principle was instrumental in ending this system. These rulings essentially turned state senates into little more than smaller versions of each state's house of representatives. See the US Supreme Court ruling *Reynolds v. Sims*, 377 U.S. 533 (1964).

low-population states *can* muster up enough votes to defeat the legislation.

The reason schemes like these are employed is to lessen the odds that certain portions of the country—and their economic and cultural interests—becomes a "permanent minority" in which voters are at the mercy of a voting majority from other parts of the country. Those who created the US Congress feared that a significant minority-majority imbalance would lead to national division, political instability, and even civil war.

Naturally, systems like these give power to a relatively small number of voters from small cantons, provinces, or states which allows them to exercise some degree of veto power over majority-supported legislation. For example, if a double majority system were employed in US presidential elections, a president could win an overwhelming majority in the popular vote, but be defeated by a coalition of small-state voters who are able to deny the needed majorities from twenty-six of the fifty states.

Those who support "one man, one vote" schemes oppose these anti-majoritarian measures.

Why Big and Powerful States and Regions Must Be Restrained

Switzerland, however, provides us insights into why simple majorities tend to be a problem. The Swiss confederation is a conglomeration of regions and cities with varying interests depending on the linguistic, religious, and cultural preferences of the population in each area. Some areas are majority Catholic and some are majority Protestant. Some areas are French speaking, and other areas are German or Italian speaking.

These differences were even more significant in the past, so the confederation was designed with some anti-majoritarian measures to prevent any small number of highly populated regions from steamrolling over the rest of the country. If, say, the German-speaking cantons became very populous, then a system based on simple majorities would mean that the German-speakers could force their preferences on everyone else. The same might be said if one religious group gained a majority.

What the "one man, one vote" advocates would have us believe, however, is that there is no need to balance these interests. In their view, if there are more pro-German voters in Switzerland, then so be it: everyone must now do what the German-speaking majority says.

Applied to the US, we see this frequently pushed by Progressives: the federalist measures designed to provide additional voting power to smaller states are denounced as "undemocratic" and we're told that if Californians and New Yorkers have an overwhelming number of votes, then that's just tough luck for everyone else. The minority must do what the majority says, even if those people have very different interests from the majorities in New York or California.

The way the Left shunts the anti-majoritarian argument aside is by insisting that there aren't any real differences between people in, say, South Dakota, and people in New Jersey. We are all "Americans." If there *are* differences, we are told, it is because people in South Dakota are backward troglodytes and their opinions shouldn't matter. This problem is solved by forcing "one man, one vote" on everyone so that South Dakotans' "unacceptable" political views are neutralized by far larger majorities in faraway cities.

Historically, such majoritarian claims would have been regarded as out-of-touch with reality. In the early twentieth century, for instance, no one denied that there were significant cultural differences between the prohibitionist Protestants of New England and the "wet" Catholics and Lutherans of the Great Lakes region. Even setting aside religious or ethnic differences, various regions of the nation had very different economic needs depending on what industries—agricultural, maritime, or manufacturing—were dominant in the region. It was recognized that agricultural areas ought to be able to offer legislative resistance to new laws designed to favor manufacturers at the expense of farmers. In case an accident of history occurred by which one group became more populous than the other, many thought it would be prudent to put safeguards in place to prevent one region from dominating the other.

Chinese Voters Would Out-Vote Everyone Else

This fundamental principle can be more easily illustrated in a hypothetical confederation with China as a member. Suppose that in twenty years, some groups of elites in eastern Asia suggest it would be a great idea to form a confederation of states from the region: the United States of East Asia (USEA). It would include China, South Korea, Japan, Vietnam, and Indonesia. This new union could be put together to facilitate free trade, free migration, and to generally increase economic prosperity and peaceful multilateralism.

How should the governance of this organization be organized? Using a unicameral legislature predicated on "one man, one vote" presents an obvious problem: the Chinese would obviously out-vote all the other countries on a regular basis. Even if South Korea, Indonesia, Vietnam, and Japan all voted together as a block, their relatively small population sizes could not possibly allow them to veto pro-China measures pushed by a majority of Chinese voters. Because of China's size, any other members of the confederation would quickly realize that the USEA was really just a union dominated by China most of the time.

On the other hand, a remedy *could* lie in creating requirements for double majorities or in assigning equal representation to all members in a senate. This would moderate China's power. If these steps were taken, though, the "one man, one vote" advocates would object and insist that China's dominance is perfectly fine because all the voters deserve equal representation and it would be "unfair" to give Japanese voters the same number of votes in the USEA senate as China.

Moreover, the "one man, one vote" advocates—were they to use the same arguments used in the US—would claim that the people of Japan and Indonesia might be unwilling to live by "the will of the majority" among "all voters" in the USEA. Insisting on anti-majoritarian measures, we may be told, just illustrates how backward and undemocratic those Japanese and Indonesians are. "Democracy" demands that every *voter*, whether Chinese, Japanese, or Vietnamese must count equally.

Clearly, such a situation would quickly lead to the dissolution of the USEA, whether peacefully or through violence. Yes, it's true that the cultural differences between people in New York and people in Utah are not as stark as the differences between the Chinese and the Japanese. But the fundamental principles behind the need for federalism in the USEA and in the USA are the same.

The French Example

Nevertheless, the "one man, one vote" idea endures, and has done so for centuries. It is tied to notions of a "general will" and the idea that "the people" (vaguely conceived) embodies the lifeblood of a nation-state. This can be traced back to the French Enlightenment and the radicals of the French Revolution.

Unlike liberal democratic notions of a decentralized, varied, and largely autonomous group of independent populations, the French revolutionary ideal of mass democracy required a version of democracy that was centralized, authoritarian, and heedless of the needs of various minorities. This became feasible in France thanks to centuries of political centralization imposed by French monarchs in the decades and centuries before the Revolution.[2] Due to the fact that France already had a strong and centralized state, French democracy was national in nature, and was based on the ideal of a single, democratic mass. Few constitutional provisions survived to check the power of the central state. Elections thus became a high-stakes matter of seizing control of a state apparatus over a single vast territory.

---

[2]Murray N. Rothbard, *Economic Thought Before Adam Smith* (Auburn, Ala.: Mises Institute, 2006), p. 201. Rothbard credits French absolutism with laying the groundwork for the French Revolution by centralizing French political power in the hands of the central state, controlled by the monarch. Rothbard writes:

> The sixteenth century French legalists also systematically tore down the legal rights of all corporations or organizations which, in the Middle Ages, had stood between the individual and the state. There were no longer any intermediary or feudal authorities. The king is absolute over these intermediaries, and makes or breaks them at will.

Rousseau's Model of Mass Democracy

It is a great irony that much of the inspiration for France's national democracy came from Switzerland itself. Jean-Jacques Rousseau, who exerted great influence on French ideas of democracy and the "general will," formed many of his ideas about democracy from his experiences in the relatively democratic Republic of Geneva. Born in Geneva to a family with voting rights, Rousseau appears to have internalized a somewhat idealized view of how Genevan democracy worked. Genevan democracy, of course, functioned on a very small scale, and it worked fairly well.

In his essay "The Background of the French Revolution," Lord Acton discussed how Rousseau's idealized views of democracy were affected by his positive experiences in Geneva:

> Rousseau was the citizen of a small republic, consisting of a single town, and he professed to have applied its example to the government of the world. It was Geneva, not as he saw it, but as he extracted its essential principle....The idea was that the grown men met in the market place, like the peasants of Glarus under their trees, to manage their affairs, making and unmaking officials, conferring and revoking powers. They were equal, because every man had exactly the same right to defend his interest by the guarantee of his vote. The welfare of all was safe in the hands of all, for they had not the separate interests that are bred by the egotism of wealth, nor the exclusive views that come from a distorted education. All being equal in power and similar in purpose, there can be no just cause why some should move apart and break into minorities.[3]

To assume, however, that the same situation is achievable at the scale of the French republic with nearly 30 million people is a blunder of impressive size. The reasons for this are well explained by Acton:

> Now the most glaring and familiar fact in history shows that the direct self-government of a town cannot be extended over

---

[3]John Dahlberg-Acton, "The Background of the French Revolution," in *Essays on Freedom and Power*, ed. Gertrude Himmelfarb (Boston: The Beacon Press, 1949), p. 264.

an empire. It is a plan that scarcely reaches beyond the next par-
ish. Either one district will be governed by another, or both by
somebody else chosen for the purpose. Either plan contradicts first
principles. Subjection is the direct negation of democracy; representation is the indirect. So that an Englishman underwent bondage to parliament as much as Lausanne to Berne or as America to
England if it had submitted to taxation, and by law recovered his
liberty but once in seven years. Consequently Rousseau, still faith-
ful to Swiss precedent as well as to the logic of his own theory, was
a federalist. In Switzerland, when one half of a canton disagrees
with the other, or the country with the town, it is deemed natural
that they should break into two, that the general will may not
oppress minorities. This multiplication of self-governing communities was admitted by Rousseau as a preservative of unanimity on
one hand, and of liberty on the other.[4]

Acton understood that protection of freedom lies in division,
decentralization, and the liberation of minorities. For Rousseau,
however, his ostensible federalism was no match for the idea of a
national will of the people. Any idea of Swiss-style federalism collapsed under the fervor for a single national legislature that could
impose the wishes of all the "French nation" to every corner of the
Republic's jurisdiction.

After all, why divide up the democratic mass if "the people" as
a whole are never wrong? "Rousseau's most advanced point was
the doctrine that the people are infallible," Acton wrote. "[French
churchman Pierre] Jurieu had taught that they can do no wrong:
Rousseau added that they are positively in the right."

Unfortunately, this ideal has never lost its appeal to many, and it
continues to plague American politics with the idea that a "will of the
people" can be realized in large scale elections across populations of
tens of millions. After all, the abandonment of locally-based democracy is not just a problem at the federal level. The state of California
today has more people than all of France during the revolution. New
York, Texas, and Florida are not far behind. All of these states are
controlled by unitary governments lacking provisions that temper

---

[4]Ibid., p. 265.

democracy and protect minorities. Such a state of affairs would be unrecognizable to the Americans of the nineteenth century. By their standards, the US has become a country of mega-states, mass democracy, and enormous republics that Rousseau might have looked on with approval.

15

Democracy Doesn't Work Unless It's Done Locally

n 2018, legislators in Iceland proposed a ban on circumcision of boys. For supporters this was a slam-dunk. Supporters viewed circumcision as a form a child abuse, and there was no down side to the legislation.[1]

For some people in the minority, however, a ban on circumcision might bring lasting damage in terms of abuses against human rights. For example, a ban on circumcision is a de facto ban on Judaism, at least of the orthodox variety.

This fact is not enough to deter some supporters of the circumcision ban, and the Icelandic legislation "insists the 'rights of the child' always exceed the 'right of the parents to give their children guidance when it comes to religion'."

Iceland is not alone in considering laws that pit the majority against the allegedly barbaric practices of a minority group.[2] In the

[1]Tom Embury-Dennis, "Iceland MPs propose ban on circumcision of boys," *Independent*, February 1, 2018, https://www.independent.co.uk/news/world/europe/iceland-circumcision-ban-boys-islam-judaism-religion-medical-reasons-muslim-jewish-a8188701.html.
[2]Catholic News Service, "Some Chinese Catholics see restrictions as new

151

Netherlands, for example, animal rights activists are hard at work trying to outlaw kosher and halal meats.[3] Meanwhile, in Quebec, lawmakers have prohibited the use of head coverings by—presumably Muslim—women in certain public places.[4]

Nor is the circumcision debate limited to Iceland. Male circumcision has been on shaky legal ground in Germany in recent years where a court banned the practice in 2012.[5] Perhaps recognizing that banning Judaism could look bad for modern German claims of "tolerance," lawmakers intervened to allow the practice again.

For the subjects of this regulation, the activities being targeted are no mere preferences. They touch on fundamental values, and they present a clear conflict with other value systems. In cases such as these, where there is no apparent room for compromise, whose values ought to prevail?

Democracy Doesn't Settle Cultural Disputes

Throughout most of the West, of course, we're all taught from an early age that democracy will allow everything to work itself out. The parties in conflict will enter into "dialogue," will arrive at a "compromise" and then everyone will be happy and at peace in the end.

---

religion rules take effect," *National Catholic Reporter*, February 8, 2018, https://www.ncronline.org/news/world/some-chinese-catholics-see-restrictions-new-religion-rules-take-effect. Chinese communist officials have taken this a step further by banning children from churches and taking other measures to "restric[t] children from joining Christian groups and attending religious activities."

[3]Nina Siegal, "New Slaughtering Rules Pit Dutch Religious Freedoms Against Animal Rights," *The New York Times*, December 31, 2017, https://www.nytimes.com/2017/12/31/world/europe/netherlands-kosher-halal-animal- rights.html.

[4]Vipal Monga, "Quebec's Law on Facial Veils Fuels Fierce Debate," *The Wall Street Journal*, January 25, 2018, https://www.wsj.com/articles/quebecs-law-on-facial-veils-fuels-fierce-debate-1516876200.

[5]Raphael Ahren, "Three months after circumcision ban, German government to legalize rite," *The Times of Israel*, October 2012, https://www.timesofisrael.com/three-months-after-local-court-banned-circumcisions-german-government-to-legalize-rite/.

But, that's not how it works in real life. While there are some areas for compromise that can be found around the edges of issues such as moral values and ethnic identity, the fact is that in the end, kosher meats are either legal or they're not. Circumcision is either legal or it's not. Abortion is either legal or it's not. Transgender "transition" surgeries for children are either legal or they're not.

After all, if one group of people believe that a 3-month-old fetus is a parasite that has trespassed against the mother, those people are going to find little room for compromise with a group of people who think the same fetus is a person deserving legal protection.

Similar dynamics are present in cases involving animal rights, circumcision, and headscarves. One side thinks that their side is the only acceptable option for virtuous, well-adjusted people. "Virtue," of course, can be defined any number of ways. Some are so blinded by their cultural biases, in fact, that they even conclude that no "civilized" person could possibly believe that, say, circumcision is anything other than a barbaric practice. Those who continue to believe in such things, it is believed, must therefore be forced "into the 21st century" by the coercive power of the state. Their religious beliefs, as Hillary Clinton demanded in 2015, "have to be changed."[6]

In any case, democracy offers no solution in addressing profound cultural differences among the residents of a single political jurisdiction. When populations with sharply differing world views must exist under a single regime, voting resolves nothing, and one side will ultimately impose its preferred policies on the other side. Noncompliance will bring down the full weight of the law, the police, and all the coercive institutions the state frequently employs. Most likely,

---

[6]Susan Jones, "Clinton: 'Deep-Seated Cultural Codes, Religious Beliefs… Have to Be Changed'," *CNSNews*, April 27, 2015, https://cnsnews.com/news/article/susan-jones/clinton-deep-seated-cultural-codes-religious-beliefshave-be-changed. According to Clinton: "Yes, we've cut the maternal mortality rate in half, but far too many women are still denied critical access to reproductive health care and safe childbirth. All the laws we've passed don't count for much if they're not enforced. Rights have to exist in practice, not just on paper. Laws have to be backed up with resources and political will. And deep-seated cultural codes, religious beliefs, and structural biases have to be changed."

the majority will end up winning, and the minority will ultimately be powerless to resist.

These problems also exist under *all* types of regimes, including authoritarian, non-democratic regimes. But anti-democrats often freely admit that the state is using force to support one side over the other. Democrats, on the other hand, often prefer to indulge in comforting fictions, and politely refrain from acknowledging that democracies can just as often produce disgruntled minority groups locked out of power by the majority.

In these cases, the only just and peaceful answer lies in dividing political jurisdictions in such a way that minority groups can separate themselves from the majority and thus attain a greater level of self-government and self-determination.

Majority Rule: Conquest and Colonialism by Other Means

In his work on nationalism, Ludwig von Mises examined the fundamental problem that arises when various groups with different value systems live under a single unitary state. Even when there are certain theoretical guarantees for minority groups, the political reality is that groups with minority beliefs are at the mercy of the majority. This is true in matters of conflicting ethnic groups and religions, but is also applicable to any number of groups with conflicting values.

Joseph Salerno sums up Mises's thought:

Mises maintains that two or more "nations" cannot peacefully coexist under a unitary democratic government. National minorities in a democracy are "completely politically powerless" because they have no chance of peacefully influencing the majority linguistic group. The latter represents "a cultural circle that is closed" to minority nationalities and whose political ideas are "thought, spoken, and written in a language that they do not understand." Even where proportional representation prevails, the national minority "still remains excluded from collaboration in political life." According to Mises, because the minority has no prospect of one day attaining power, the activity of its representatives "remains limited from the beginning to fruitless criticism...that...can lead to no political goal." Thus, concludes Mises, even if the member of the minority nation, "according to the letter of the law, be a citizen with full rights…in truth he is politically without rights, a second-class citizen, a pariah."

Mises characterizes majority rule as a form of colonialism from the point of view of the minority nation in a polyglot territory: "[It] signifies something quite different here than in nationally uniform territories; here, for a part of the people, it is not popular rule but foreign rule." Peaceful liberal nationalism therefore is inevitably stifled in polyglot territories governed by a unitary state, because, Mises argues, "democracy seems like oppression to the minority. Where only the choice is open oneself to suppress or be suppressed, one easily decides for the former." Thus, for Mises, democracy means the same thing for the minority as "subjugation under the rule of others."[7]

Those on the winning side, of course, don't see any problem here. What the minority thinks of as "oppression" is really—according to the winners—just "modernization," "progress," "decency," "common sense," or simply "the will of the majority." The fact that the enforcement of that will of the majority is founded on state violence is of little concern.

The Solution: Secession and Decentralization

Historically, however, local autonomy and local self-governance has long been used by regimes for purposes of calming ethnic tensions, preventing rebellions, or encouraging economic development. Confederations like Switzerland explicitly employ a decentralized structure so as to avoid conflict between religious and linguistic groups. This tradition of self-government goes far deeper into European culture, however. For example, during the Middle Ages and Early Modern period, residents of towns in Europe were frequently

---

[7]Joseph T. Salerno, "Mises on Nationalism, the Right of Self-Determination, and the Problem of Immigration," *Mises Wire*, March 28, 2017, https://mises.org/wire/mises-nationalism-right-self-determination-and-problem-immigration.

granted self-government separate from the surrounding populations and districts ruled directly by the monarch or by local nobles. This was done in recognition of the fact that the populations in the towns had interests quite different from those in the countryside. The recognition of this separateness of the towns was reflected in so-called "German Town Law." These separate legal codes—also known as Magdeburg law or Lübeck law—provided for self-governance in matters of local economic regulation and all the usual ordinances associated with municipal governments. So long as these cities paid their taxes and did not pose a geopolitical threat to the dominant princes, they were left alone. Often, this self-governance also took on an ethnic and linguistic color as many of these towns were populated largely by ethnic Germans living in regions populated largely by other ethnic groups.

Similar arrangements were also often enjoyed by Jews in the Polish-Lithuanian Commonwealth of the Early Modern period. Jewish communities, known as *kehilot*, generally were granted self-government, and a national parliament of these communities—the Va'ad Arba' Aratzot—met to address the needs of the Jewish communities at large. (Notably, as the Polish state went into decline and gave way to Russian, Austrian, and Prussian dominance, these self-governing Jewish communities were reined in.)

The tolerance extended to these minority groups was not necessarily granted out of enlightened motives, of course. These were a recognition by many princes and rulers that self-government helped to neutralize conflict between majorities and minorities. Moreover, given that many regimes were more geared toward addressing wars and other geopolitical concerns, it was often best to simply allow many domestic groups the option of self-governance so long as these groups were not problematic for international relations.

Unfortunately, the prudence and tolerance that undergirds this line of thinking has been lost in much of the modern political world, and it is now generally accepted that the modern democratic state must apply universal policy across an entire national population. Mises, who was clearly knowledgeable about the history of central and eastern Europe, likely was well aware of the longer tradition of local self-governance, and saw its benefits.

Mises—who was himself a democrat—understood that democratic elections offered no real solution to the problem of political minorities. For Mises, populations—regardless of whether they live within a democratic system or not—must not be forced into states where they will never be able to exercise self-determination due to the presence of a more powerful majority. On a practical level then, populations in regions, cities, and villages within existing states must be free to form their own states if need be, or join other states with friendlier majorities.

Mises explicitly recognized the benefits of this in maintaining the peace. In *Liberalism*, he writes that if "the inhabitants of a particular territory" seeks to leave one political jurisdiction and join another—or just remain independent—"their wishes are to be respected and complied with. *This is the only feasible and effective way of preventing revolutions and civil and international wars*" (emphasis added).[8]

According to Mises, without this option of peaceful separation, the permanent minority—should it wish to advance any efforts at self-determination—is left with few choices in the long run other than violent separation or rebellion. Additionally, in order to accommodate the realities of constantly-changing populations, borders and boundaries must change over time in order to minimize the number of people within minority populations with little to no say in national governments controlled by hostile majorities.

In Mises's vision, there is no perfect solution. There will always be some minority groups that are at odds with the ruling majority. But, when states are smaller, more numerous, and more diverse in terms of policy, communities and individuals stand a better chance of finding a state in which their values match up with the majority. Large unitary states, however, offer exactly the opposite: less choice, less diversity, and fewer chances to exercise self-determination.

---

[8]Ludwig von Mises, *Liberalism: A Socio-Economic Exposition* (Kansas City, Mo.: Sheed Andrews and McMeel, 1962), p. 109.

Part III
Lessons from America's Past, and Strategies for the Future

16

How Early Americans Decentralized Military Power

Since the Second World War, the American regime has greatly expanded military spending and military operations far above and beyond what had been the case before the war. Many view this as a positive development, and those who favor an active and interventionist posture for American military affairs have frequently criticized American policy before the war as "isolationist." More specifically, critics of pre-war policy contend the US lacked the military spending, personnel, and materiel necessary to meet the needs of defense for the United States in an increasingly globalized world.

The charge of "isolationism," however, rather exaggerates the US's military posture before the twentieth century, and it is not the case that American policymakers were especially pacifistic before the Second World War. This can be seen in a multitude of military interventions carried out by the US regime in earlier decades. We can point to full-scale wars, of course, like the First World War and the Spanish-American War, but we can also note smaller-scale interventions such as those in Korea (1888–89, 1894–96) the Philippines (1898–1946), and a *multitude* of interventions in Latin America dating back to the 1840s.

What was different about the nineteenth century, however, was that land-based military forces tended to be much more temporary, *ad hoc*, and limited in size. This was by design.

As with most other governmental prerogatives, the federal government's military powers were decentralized, with most military power to be held within the member states themselves. Many of the early American liberals assumed it was best to decentralize military power to lessen the chances of abuse by a central government.

A Limit on Military Capability
as a Limit on Regime Power

The idea that a regime's military forces—especially its land-based forces—ought to be restrained was a key component of the ideological program of the classical liberals who had fought in the American Revolution.

As Americans debated what ought to be the full extent of federal power, many Americans continued to fear that a strong national government would simply replace the British crown in terms of military might and coercive power.

These fears date back at least to the English Civil War, and the time of the Levellers, whom Murray Rothbard described as "the world's first self-consciously libertarian movement."[1] By the 1640s, Leveller reformers were calling for a decentralized militia system which would lessen the power of the king in domestic affairs. In *The Levellers: Radical Political Thought in the English Revolution*, Rachel Foxley writes:

> In the Third Agreement of the People, in May 1649, the Levellers proposed that armed forces were to be raised strictly by local divisions, and officered by men elected locally; only the general officers were to be appointed by Parliament. [John] Wildman was to express similar views in more specifically republican terms in the

---

[1]Roberta A. Modugno, "England's Levellers: The World's First Libertarian Movement," *Mises Wire*, March 27, 2014, https://mises.org/library/englands-levellers-worlds-first-libertarian-movement-0.

1650s, opposing "mercenary" armies in favour of the people being "masters of their own Arms"...[2]

The years of Civil War would be disorienting in terms of military power, but, as British historian Marcus Cunliffe explains in his history of American military institutions:

> At the restoration of the Stuarts in 1660, both Charles II and Parliament would for different reasons have liked to be rid of the Cromwellian legacy of the New Model Army. But some troops were needed to keep order. A compromise was reached. First, a small regular force was to be maintained: this was the actual foundation of the British standing army. Second, there was to be a nationwide militia, composed of civilians who would—as in earlier days—be summoned in time of need. The militia, however, was to be under civil law, and to be organized locally by the lord lieutenant of each county. It was thus decentralized and divorced from royal control.[3]

Cunliffe further explains that later American attitudes toward a standing army were adopted nearly wholesale from earlier English attitudes about militias and civil control of the military. These attitudes can be found in the Declaration of Independence itself which lists among its grievances the fact that the king "has kept among us, in times of peace, Standing Armies without the Consent of our legislatures...[and] has affected to render the Military independent of and superior to the Civil Power."

By the time of the American constitutional debates, these concerns were addressed in part by the adoption of what is now known as the Second Amendment of the United States Constitution. Anti-Federalists and other Americans fearful of centralized power in the US government designed the amendment to guarantee that the states would be free to raise and train their own militias as a defense against federal power. These militias were also a means of keeping a

---

[2]Quoted in Ryan McMaken, "The Origins of 'Militia' in the Second Amendment—It's Not About Slavery, *Mises Wire*, April 2, 2018, https://mises.org/wire/origins-militia-second-amendment-its-not-about-slavery.

[3]Marcus Cunliffe, *Soldiers and Civilians: The Martial Spirit in America, 1775–1865* (Boston: Little, Brown, and Company, 1968), p. 32.

defensive military force available to Americans, but which remained outside the direct control of the federal government.

In his book *Eagle and Sword: The Federalists and the Creation of the Military Establishment in America, 1783–1802*, Richard Kohn writes:

> No principle of government was more widely understood or more completely accepted by the generation of Americans that established the United States than the danger of a standing army in peacetime. Because a standing army represented the ultimate in uncontrolled and controllable power, any nation that maintained permanent forces surely risked the overthrow of legitimate government and the introduction of tyranny and despotism.[4]

We can see this plainly in the speeches and writings of the Anti-Federalists like Patrick Henry. We see it in the more moderate attendees of the constitutional convention as well, such as George Mason, who wrote "When once a standing army is established in any country, the people lose their liberty."[5]

These ideas were further developed at the Virginia ratifying convention where Patrick Henry mocked the idea that liberties could be preserved by simply "assembling the people." Without locally controlled military might, Henry noted, federal force could destroy the independence of the state governments. Similarly, George Mason concluded that the "militia...is our ultimate safety. We can have no security without it."

As historian Leon Friedman concludes, "the people organized in the state militias were regarded as a counterforce against the threat that the regular army could be used as an instrument of oppression, and service in the militia was a right of the citizen that could not be transgressed by the federal government."[6]

---

[4]Quoted in Anthony A. Peacock, *Vindicating the Commercial Republic: The Federalist on Union, Enterprise, and War* (Lanham, Maryland: Lexington Books, 2018), p. 163.

[5]George Mason, "Debate in Virginia Ratifying Convention," June 14, 1788, https://press-pubs.uchicago.edu/founders/print_documents/a1_8_12s27.html.

[6]Leon Friedman, "Conscription and the Constitution: The Original Understanding," 67 *Michigan Law Review* 1493 (1969): 1536.

Even after the adoption of the new constitution, opposition to a powerful federal military continued. Congress opposed not only attempts to increase the size of the professional US army much beyond 1,000 men, but also opposed attempts to mandate any specific training in a "federally organized militia system." In the end, opposition to federal control of military affairs meant training of militias was "left entirely to the states."[7]

This is understandable given the long tradition of the "unorganized militia" in American history. This notion was recognized by policymakers even before ratification of the federal constitution, as noted by legal historian David Yassky:

> As we have seen, in practice Founding-era militias were far from universal, but in the Founders' conceptual framework the militia consisted of the mass of ordinary citizens, trained to arms and available to serve at the call of the state. As George Mason put it: "Who are the militia? They consist now of the whole people, except [for] a few public officers"....When the Second Congress sought to exercise its constitutional authority to "provide for organizing, arming and disciplining the Militia," it directed "each and every free able-bodied white male citizen of the respective states [except for persons exempted under state law and certain other exempted classes]...who is...of the age of eighteen years, and under the age of forty-five years" to enroll in the militia of their states. Or as Patrick Henry declared at the Virginia ratifying convention: "The great object is, that every man be armed."[8]

Far from eschewing the idea of military defense altogether, many states went to great lengths to ensure a large number of armed men were potentially available in case of invasion or general disorder.

For example, an 1894 collection of texts from state constitutions shows that no fewer than 22 state constitutions contained language along the lines of "the militia of the State shall consist

---

[7]Ibid., 1538.
[8]David Yassky, "The Second Amendment: Structure, History, and Constitutional Change," 99 *Michigan Law Review* 588 (2000): 624.

of all able-bodied male residents of the State, between the ages of eighteen and forty-five years."[9,10]

To ensure a ready availability of men used to handling firearms, these constitutional provisions are often accompanied by state guarantees of a right to keep and bear arms similar to the 1780 Massachusetts declaration of rights which states:

> The people have a right to keep and to bear arms for the common defence. And as, in time of peace, armies are dangerous to liberty, they ought not to be maintained without the consent of the legislature; and the military power shall always be held in an exact subordination to the civil authority, and be governed by it.[11]

Ideally, each state would have its own "unorganized militia" of residents who could "aid...the civil power" in case of civil unrest or invasion. American policymakers took these measures as part of an effort to ensure the federal government would not overwhelm state and local governments.

For a long time, the strategy worked. Throughout most of the nineteenth century, land-based military power continued to be heavily decentralized among the American member states and their militias.

The federal government directly controlled only a small force of professional federal officers and enlisted men. This meant that if the federal government wished to carry out any sizable military operations, it required the consent of the member states and their governments. Without this consent, it was impossible to "call forth" the militias for federal purposes.

---

[9] *The Convention Manuel of the Sixth New York State Constitutional Convention, 1894* (Albany, N.Y.: The Argus Company, 1894).

[10] Texts declaring all able-bodied adults as members of the militia were, in the late nineteenth century, found in Alabama, Arkansas, Florida, Idaho, Illinois, Indiana, Iowa, Kansas, Kentucky, Michigan, Mississippi, Missouri, Montana, North Carolina, Ohio, Oregon, Pennsylvania, South Dakota, Virginia, Washington, and Wyoming.

[11] Massachusetts Declaration of Rights, Article 17 (1780), http://blog.mass. gov/masslawlib/legal-history/massachusetts-declaration-of-rights-article-17/.

Member State Vetoes on "Calling Forth the Militia"

While the Constitution of 1787 does not explicitly provide for a member-state veto on the federal use of militias, there were historically both statutory and customary barriers to presidents drawing upon local troops without the consent of member-state governors and legislatures.

In some cases, these member-state governments asserted control over their militia troops when federal orders conflicted with the agenda of the member states themselves. For example, during the War of 1812, the governor of Vermont, Martin Chittenden, attempted to recall Vermont troops that had been federalized by the US government and sent to New York. Chittenden declared "[It] has been ordered from our frontiers to the defence of a neighboring state...[and] placed under the command, and at the disposal of, an officer of the United States, out of the jurisdiction or control of the executive of this state."[12]

During the same conflict, the state legislature of Connecticut issued a declaration passed by both houses: "it must not be forgotten, that the state of Connecticut is a FREE, SOVEREIGN, and INDEPENDENT state; that the United States are a confederacy of states; that we are a confederated and not a consolidated republic" (emphasis in original).[13]

At the time, the governor of Connecticut refused to comply with a requisition of troops from the United States Secretary of War. The governor condemned the federal attempt at nationalizing the militia and wrote: "By the principles of the proposed plan...our sons, our brothers and friends are made liable to be delivered, against their will and by force, to the marshals and recruiting officers of the United States, to be employed not for our defence, but for the conquest of Canada..."[14] The state assembly concluded that the federal demands

---

[12]Jeff Taylor, *Politics on a Human Scale: The American Tradition of Decentralism* (Lanham, Maryland: Lexington Books, 2013), p. 60.

[13]Ibid.

[14]William Chauncey Fowler, *Local Law in Massachusetts and Connecticut, Historically Considered* (Albany, N.Y.: Joel Munsell, 1872), p. 93.

were "not only intolerably oppressive, but subversive of the rights and liberties of the state, and the freedom, sovereignty, and independence of the same, and inconsistent with the principles of the constitution of the United States."[15]

According to William Chauncey Fowler, writing in his book *Local Law in Massachusetts and Connecticut*:

> The Governor of Connecticut took the ground that, by the constitution of the United States, the entire control of the militia is given to the state, except in certain specified cases, namely: to execute the laws of the union, the suppress insurrection, and to repel invasions, and he contended that neither of these cases actually existed. He also took the ground that the militia could not be compelled to serve under any other than their own officers, with the exception of the president himself, when personally in the field.[16]

The state legislature concurred.

Kentucky Declares Neutrality

Another notable case of a state asserting control over its own military resources is Kentucky's insistence on neutrality in the early days of the American Civil War. By 1860, demographic and economic changes in Kentucky had made it a semi-industrialized state with a declining reliance on the slave economy.[17] Kentucky had close economic ties with both Northern and Southern states. Kentucky governor Beriah Magoffin opposed secession for Kentucky. Yet he also opposed military efforts to force the secessionist states back into the Union. That is, he was unwilling to directly support either the Union or the Confederacy, and asserted neutrality in the war. Magoffin announced "I will send not a man nor a dollar for the wicked purpose of subduing my sister Southern States," and he

---

[15]Ibid.

[16]Ibid.

[17]Kent Masterson Brown, *The Civil War in Kentucky: Battle for the Bluegrass State* (Mason City, Iowa: Savas Publishing, 2000), p. 5.

refused a federal demand for four regiments from Kentucky to be added to the Union army.[18]

Magoffin was not alone in neutralist views, and former Kentucky Senator Archibald Dixon urged local citizens "to stand firm with her sister Border States in the centre of the Republic to calm the distracted sections."[19] By this, Dixon claimed, Kentucky "saves the Union and frowns down Secession."[20] Similarly, an assembly of voters in Louisville convened a public meeting on the matter and concluded it was the "duty of Kentucky...to maintain her present independent position, taking sides not with the [Lincoln] Administration, nor with the seceding states, but with the Union against them both."[21] Reflecting on the extent to which Kentucky had separated itself from both the North and the South during this period, Lowell Harrison has suggested that, at the time, "a bewildered observer from abroad might well have concluded that the United States had become three countries: the Union, the Confederacy, and Kentucky."[22]

Predictably, Lincoln himself—who had concluded he must avoid military intervention to force Kentucky's compliance—took a dim view of Kentucky's neutrality, declaring the doctrine of "armed neutrality" to be "disunion completed," while neutrality "recognizes no fidelity to the Constitution, no obligation to maintain the Union" and as "treason in effect."[23]

---

[18]Clint Johnson, *"A Vast and Fiendish Plot": The Confederate Attack on New York City* (New York: Kensington Publishing, 2010), p. 90.

[19]James A. Rawley, *A Lincoln Dialogue*, ed. William G. Thomas (Lincoln: University of Nebraska Press, 2014), p. 139.

[20]Quoted in Frank Moore, ed., *Rebellion Record: a Diary of American Events: Documents and Narratives*, vol. 1, http://www.perseus.tufts.edu/hopper/text.jsp?doc= Perseus%3Atext%3A2001.05.0135%3Apage%3D76.

[21]Jerome A. Watrous, ed., *The Union Army, A History of Military Affairs in the Loyal States 1861–65* (Madison, Wis.: Federal Publishing Company, 1908), p. 286.

[22]Lowell Harrison, *The Civil War in Kentucky* (Lexington: University Press of Kentucky, 1975), p. 9.

[23]Abraham Lincoln, Message to Congress in Special Session, July 4, 1861,

Lincoln would eventually obtain political support from Kentucky, but not because he won the constitutional or legal argument. Eventually, Unionists took control of the state government and sided with the Union over the confederacy. This ended the debate.

Nevertheless, the Kentucky case merely continued the established practice of state governments vetoing federal use of state militias and military resources. In the case of Kentucky, the assertion that state governments could prevent federalization of local troops had worked as intended: Unionists—both in Washington and locally—were forced to win political support for the Northern side among Kentuckians before state resources could be used to prosecute the war.

Technically, Lincoln faced this problem in every northern state, although most state governments willingly sent state-organized troops to the war effort because they were ideologically aligned with the anti-secession movement. Had Lincoln failed to win political support from the individual states, however, he would have lacked the resources necessary to prosecute the war. At the time, the federal government simply lacked the resources necessary to carry on a large military operation of the type needed to invade the Southern states.

The Twentieth Century: State Militias Nationalized

By the early twentieth century, after a long period during which state governments exercised some level of control over the deployment of state militias, the federal government began to consolidate control over military resources in the states.

The first large step toward consolidation came in the form of the Militia Act of 1903 which for the first time began the use of the phrase "National Guard" in federal statutes. This new legislation also paved the way for the use of National Guard units to be used outside the territory of the United States, with a 1906 amendment specifically

---

https://www.whatsoproudlywehail.org/curriculum/the-american-calendar/ message-to-congress-in-special-session.

creating a provision for the use of militia units "either within or without the territory of the United States."[24]

This provision was later contested on constitutional grounds, but the Congress responded with the National Defense Act of 1916 which made it even easier for the president to call up state troops for federal purposes.

Over time, the line between state militias and federal troops became increasingly blurred, and today, with the exception of the "state defense forces" state National Guard units today do not function independently of the United States government in any meaningful way.

The final nail in the coffin of local control came in 1987 courtesy of Mississippi Congressman Gillespie Montgomery. Montgomery introduced a provision in the 1987 National Defense Authorization Act which specifically states that "The consent of a Governor... may not be withheld (in whole or in part) with regard to active duty outside the United States, its territories, and its possessions, because of any objection to the location, purpose, type, or schedule of such active duty."

In the nineteenth century, of course, when liberal factions like the Jacksonians were in power, this measure would have been considered to be blatantly unconstitutional, unwise, and immoral. But in 1990, the US Supreme Court, reflecting dominant opinion among American politicians, sided with the Congress and ruled against attempts by governors in California and Minnesota to stop deployments of state troops overseas.[25]

Thus, the Montgomery Amendment ended any remaining ability of states to veto federal use of member-state "militias." By the mid-twentieth century, though, state militias had already been dwarfed

---

[24] *University of Illinois Studies on the Social Sciences: War Powers of the Executive in the United States* 9, nos. 1–2, March–June 1920 (Urbana: University of Illinois Press), p. 133.

[25] David Evans, "Supreme Court Confirms U.S. Control Over Guard, *Chicago Tribune,* June 12, 1990, https://www.chicagotribune.com/news/ct-xpm-1990-06-12-9002170920-story.html.

by the national army and air force that could function totally independently of the American member states.

Why Military Decentralization Is Important

The Montgomery Amendment completed a long period during which a permanent "standing army" gradually replaced an earlier model of militia power decentralized among state governments. The eighteenth-century fear of centrally-controlled federal troops had given way to support for state troops that were state militias in name only, and subject primarily to federal control. The model of a decentralized army had originally been employed to limit federal military power, but physical and financial control of land-based military power is now firmly within the hands of the central government.

17

Before *Roe v. Wade*, Abortion Policy was a State and Local Matter

Some anti-abortion advocates today imagine that abortion was rare and taboo prior to *Roe vs. Wade*, the 1973 Supreme Court decision that federalized abortion law. The National Right to Life Committee (NRLC) says exactly this in its online "abortion timeline" where it states "there is evidence of a few rogue doctors and midwives performing abortions in the US as far back as the 1850s." The timeline itself does not begin until 1959, thus implying that no notable legal or legislative battle took place before the mid-twentieth century.[1]

The NRLC's version of the past, however, is very much at odds with the actual legislative history in which both abortion—and legislation impeding it—were widespread during the nineteenth century. What was different about these battles, however, was that they were waged at the state and local levels.

---

[1] "Abortion History Timeline," National Right to Life Committee, https://www.nrlc.org/archive/abortion/facts/abortiontimeline.html.

Going back to the seventeenth century, prohibitions could be found, but as Janet Farrell Brodie writes in *Contraception and Abortion in Nineteenth-Century America*: "Convictions for abortion, however, were rare. Middlesex County in Massachusetts had only four convictions for attempted abortion between 1633 and 1699."[2]

Brodie notes that technology and public knowledge related to abortion had changed significantly over time:

> How Americans learned about ways to control or prevent pregnancy was radically transformed in the decades after the 1830s by public lectures and new genres of literature giving contraceptive advice.

In consumer-driven America, this led to growing industries making contraceptive and abortion services more widely available. Brodie continues:

> Abortion instruments, like drugs, were readily available through the mails or from a variety of retail establishments, particularly drugstores, and wholesale druggists' catalogues carried a considerable variety of styles and models in uterine sounds and dilators. Newspapers regularly carried advertisements for abortion-inducing drugs.
>
> By mid century there was a growing number of professional abortionists, and not only in large cities, as W.M. Smith, a physician in the small farming town of Atkinson, Illinois (population 300) noted in 1874....Smith estimated that his town had one abortion for every ten live births.[3]

Just how widespread was abortion? Not surprisingly, nineteenth-century statistics on the matter are sparse. But, as James Mohr writes in *Abortion in America: the Origins and Evolution of National Policy, 1800–1900* a number of contemporary researchers concluded that numbers were quite high by historical standards:

> Dr. P.S. Haskell, in a report to the Medical Association of Maine..."suggest[ed] a ratio of one abortion for every six live

---

[2]Janet Farrell Brodie, *Contraception and Abortion in Nineteenth-century America* (Ithaca, N.Y.: Cornell University Press, 1997), p. 39.
[3]Ibid., p. 227.

births at a minimum."...Horace Knapp wrote in 1873, "There can be no doubt that more children are destroyed annually in their mother's womb than are born alive."...By the end of the decade of the 1870s, medical writers began to suggest earlier estimates had been, if anything, too low. In 1878 physicians testifying in the murder trial of an abortionist in southern Illinois set the ratio at 25 percent of all pregnancies...[this was followed by] still another upward revision of the Storer and Heard ratio of one abortion in every five pregnancies made by the Michigan State Board of Health two years later.

Physicians in Michigan, according to a special committee of the Board of Health, were directly aware of "seventeen abortions to every hundred pregnancies" and were also convinced that at least "as many more...never come to the physician's knowledge".... Occasionally during the 1880s a physician might estimate an abortion rate as low as "ten percent of all pregnancies," but most writers arrived at calculations of at least as high as the Michigan rate of one-third. A doctor who had practiced in Philadelphia for twenty-five years "stated as his firm conviction that more than one-half of the human family dies before it is born."[4]

Some of these figures are comparable to modern-day abortion ratios reported by the Guttmacher Institute. During the 1990s—a high-abortion period—ratios reached 25 abortions per 100 pregnancies.[5] In 2014, after several years of decline, the ratio fell to 18.8 per 100 pregnancies.

Seeking better confirmation of his historical statistics, Mohr looked to the birthrates of the time:

The record of birthrates in the United States during the nineteenth century underlies all the foregoing contemporary evidence and offer a final reason to believe that the United States experienced a great upsurge in the incidence of abortion that began around 1840 and continued roughly through the 1870s. The data are circumstantial to be sure, but striking nonetheless, especially

---

[4]James C. Mohr, *Abortion in America: The Origins and Evolution of National Policy, 1800–1900* (Oxford, U.K.: Oxford University Press, 1978), p. 81.

[5]Rachel K. Jones, "Abortion Incidence and Service Availability In the United States," 2014, https://onlinelibrary.wiley.com/doi/full/10.1363/psrh.12015.

when combined with the conclusion of modern demographers about the population trends in other societies...the average American women bore 7.04 children in 1800; 3.56 by 1900. The steepest decennial drop in this long decline, which had been a slight trough the first three decades of the century, occurred between 1840 and 1850, exactly when abortion information, abortion services, and abortion itself came out in to the open.[6]

The Legislative Response

Faced with what was apparently a period of considerable growth in abortion, many social reformers attempted to implement legislative restrictions. These legislative changes, however, were done at the state level, and were often accompanied by efforts to regulate medical procedures and facilities overall. It was the newly organized American Medical Association that led the charge in 1857. In *When Abortion Was a Crime*, Leslie Reagan notes that "Through the 1870s, regular physicians across the country worked for the passage of new criminal abortion laws. In securing criminal abortion laws, the Regulars won recognition of their particular views as well as some state control over the practice of medicine."[7]

In spite of this nationwide drive for abortion restrictions, federal law remained generally untouched. Notable exceptions were the so-called Comstock Laws which prohibited the use of the US Postal Service to send abortifacients through the mail. Note, however, that federal authority ended with the federal government's postal service. Any direct prohibition of abortion was seen as having to originate with state laws. And, when state laws were passed, enforcement was haphazard, to say the least. Reagan continues:

The underlying structure of medicine and the law at the time of the century fostered the practice of abortion everywhere. When

---

[6]Mohr, *Abortion in America*, p. 81.

[7]Leslie J. Reagan, *When Abortion Was a Crime: Women, Medicine, and Law in the United States, 1867–1973* (Berkeley: University of California Press, 1998), p. 11. "Regulars" were physicians that were usually part of the AMA mainstream, as opposed to "irregular" physicians who did not have credentials from the AMA or similar organizations.

the *Chicago Times* focused on the business of abortion, it ignored the exception in the state criminal abortion law that allowed physicians to perform therapeutic abortion. The law itself contributed to the medical practice of abortion. The Illinois abortion statute exempted "any person who procured or attempts to produce the miscarriage of any pregnant women for *bona fide* medical or surgical purposes." What constitutes a *bona fide* reason, however, was left undefined.[8]

By the 1890s, anti-abortion doctors were again attempting to re-invigorate a movement which some saw as faltering again. The second wave, as described by Reagan, also focused again on state and local laws:

The new antiabortion crusade pursued a three-pronged strategy. Medical efforts focused, first, on reeducating American women and then public about the immorality and dangers of abortion. This cultural campaign took place in physicians' offices and patients' homes during individual encounters as well and in public group forums. Second, antiabortion physicians worked internally within medical societies to eliminate abortionists from the medical profession. Third, the antiabortion campaign moved its focus from state legislatures to the local level, where the new laws were enforced. The new activists sought an alliance with the state officials in enforcing the law. Antiabortionists identified an entire group of practitioners they believed responsible for illegal abortion: immigrant midwives. The attempt by specialists in obstetrics to restrict their competitors was the most visible and public aspect of the new campaign. The purging of the profession was treated as a private problem...

Abortion was not a political issue in the sense that it has become today; it neither played a role in national presidential elections nor reached the U.S. Supreme Court. Yet during the Progressive Era, abortion became a contested issue of interest to politicians and target of new legislation at both the local and state levels.[9]

---

[8]Ibid., p. 61.
[9]Ibid., p. 81.

Recognizing the limitations of legislation to change what was widely-accepted behavior, the reformers focused often on non-governmental solutions. Nor was victory assured. While some doctors stressed the medical risks of abortion, many doctors nevertheless saw opposition to abortion as the "Christian duty" while some admitted that their patients were not necessarily open to what physicians had to say. As one Colorado doctor of the time admitted, "Some people...will laugh at the doctor for telling them that it is murder to kill an unborn infant."[10]

The Federalization of Abortion

By the mid-twentieth century, the cultural and professional factors that had driven the anti-abortion movement in the nineteenth century began to disappear. The AMA and its physicians no longer pushed for continued restrictions on abortion as they once had. Pro-abortion activists began to successfully push for the repeal of state-level restrictions.

Anti-abortion activists experienced a loss of influence with both cultural and political institutions that had driven the anti-abortion movement two generations earlier.

The Pew Research Center provides a brief history of the turning point:

In 1967, Colorado became the first state to greatly broaden the circumstances under which a woman could legally receive an abortion. By 1970, 11 additional states had made similar changes to their abortion laws and four other states—New York, Washington, Hawaii and Alaska—had completely decriminalized abortion during the early stages of pregnancy.[11]

Even into the early 1970s, abortion continued to be a state-level issue. *Roe v. Wade* changed all that. When the Supreme Court handed down the *Roe* decision in 1973, it took abortion matters out of the

---

[10]Ibid., p. 84.

[11]"A History of Key Abortion Rulings of the U.S. Supreme Court," January 16, 2013, https://www.pewforum.org/2013/01/16/a-history-of-key-abortion-rulings-of-the-us-supreme-court/.

states and placed them into the hands of federal law-enforcement agencies, federal courts, and Congress in a way that had never been done before. As is the usual modern practice in American politics, this revolutionary rewriting of the Constitution was done without a Constitutional amendment, and thus cut short any national debate that was taking place in state legislatures and local institutions.

The centralization of abortion policy also turned every national election in part into a referendum on abortion, thus raising the stakes for voters for whom abortion is an important issue. While state lawmakers were once forced to "agree to disagree" with abortion policies in other states, now the rise of nationwide abortion policy threatens to upend the preferences of local majorities whenever a change is made. No longer is it possible for voters in Texas to simply shrug and accept they can't do anything about legal abortion in California. Now, federal politics potentially poses a direct threat to each state's majority-preferred social policies. "Live and let live" is no longer an option, further raising tensions between national voting blocs and between regional populations.

18

When Immigration Policy Was Decentralized

O n nearly all sides of the immigration debate, it is generally assumed today that the federal government in the United States ought to be the final word in immigration policy. Efforts by state governments to enforce or adopt immigration policies of their own are struck down by federal courts. Interest groups repeatedly look to Congress and the White House to hand down national policy on immigration.

Federal control of immigration policy is a relatively recent development, however, and it is not until the 1880s that we see the national government displace the states as the primary enforcer of immigration law. And even then, states continued to work in cooperation with the federal government. It was not until the twentieth century that the federal government began to insist that it had a monopoly on immigration law, and that the states were excluded from exercising their own powers in the matter.

In his lengthy article on "The Lost Century of American Immigration Law" in the *Columbia Law Review*, Gerald Neuman notes that state and local law had been used to restrict migration in the North American colonies—and later the United States.[1] The legal framework of these immigration measures had their origins in English poor laws that restricted the movements of paupers, vagabonds, and other alleged undesirables. Neuman notes that after independence, local governments in many places retained control over settlement:

> After 1794 [in Massachusetts], persons newly arriving in a town became settled inhabitants if they met certain statutory criteria, such as property ownership, or if they received express permission of the town government.[2]

The idea was to prevent the permanent settlement of any persons who were likely to become reliant on local charity efforts, or who might be criminals. These restrictions, in fact, were acknowledged and written into the Articles of Confederation in which Article IV states that states retained the powers to limit the movements of "paupers, vagabonds and fugitives from justice." Neuman further contends that "Although the Constitution omits this qualification from its Privileges and Immunities Clause, the courts continued to assume that paupers had no right to travel."[3]

Historical experience in the states confirms that restrictions on free travel did not go away with the new Constitution and indeed new restrictions on incoming migrants from outside the US were introduced.

In his study on state-level immigration laws, Hidetaka Hirota focuses on state laws in Massachusetts and New York where the matter of expelling and limiting new migrants was a matter of perennial concern:

> To reduce Irish pauperism, New York and Massachusetts built upon colonial poor laws for regulating the local movement of the poor to check the landing into the state of destitute foreigners.

[1]Gerald L. Neuman, "The Lost Century of American Immigration Law (1776–1875)," *Columbia Law Review* 93, no. 8 (December 1993): 1833–1901.
[2]Ibid., p. 1848.
[3]Ibid., p. 1847.

In Massachusetts, an exceptionally strong anti-Catholic and anti-Irish tradition inspired the state legislature to go beyond merely setting entry regulations or excluding the unacceptable. Rather, Massachusetts developed laws for deporting foreign paupers already resident in the state back to Ireland or to Britain, Canada, or other American states. Between the 1830s and the early 1880s, at least 50,000 persons were removed from Massachusetts under this policy. State policies applied to all destitute foreigners, and German immigrants attracted their fair share of nativism. Those expelled from Massachusetts also included American paupers who originally came from other states. Yet it was Irish poverty that generated the principal momentum for the growth of state immigration policy.[4]

Given the fact that Boston and New York were such popular destinations for the Irish during this period, these two states were the most active in instituting immigration controls. Other states engaged in some efforts, although as Hirota notes:

...Maryland and Louisiana had little interest in restricting European immigration throughout the nineteenth century, while Pennsylvania and California failed to establish sustainable systems of immigration regulation.[5]

It was these laws that led to some of the earliest legal decisions in the US as to the role of the federal government in immigration law.

Early Supreme Court Cases

Early legal cases illustrated a reluctance on the part of the court to assert federal control of migrants. In *New York v. Miln* (1837) for example, the Court took up the matter of whether a state could require a docking ship to "to provide a list of passengers and to post security against the passengers from becoming public charges." The strategy of bonding was often used in which ship owners were forced

---

[4]Hidetaka Hirota, *Expelling the Poor: Atlantic Seaboard States and the Nineteenth-Century Origins of American Immigration Policy* (Oxford, U.K.: Oxford University Press, 2017), p. 2.

[5]Ibid., p. 3.

to post a bond under which the state could be compensated in case the new migrants arriving in said ship turned out to be criminals or paupers dependent on the state.

The court sided with the state, concluding the state was entitled "to provide precautionary measures against the moral pestilence of paupers, vagabonds, and possible convicts, as it is to guard against the physical pestilence, which may arise from unsound and infectious articles imported."[6]

However, regulation of immigrants was acceptable to the court so long as the regulation was "not a regulation of commerce, but of police."[7] That is, the court ruled to overturn the state's ability to impose what were essentially taxes on shipping, while concluding that the state and local governments nevertheless retained the right to regulate the immigrants themselves. This included the right to refuse entry to new migrants perceived to be paupers, criminals, mentally ill, or carrying communicable diseases. As Hirota recounts, these "police powers" resulted in many deportations conducted by state officials.

Moreover, in the "Passenger Cases" of 1849, the court again declined to limit state police powers in regulating immigrants.[8] The majority "consensus" which consisted of several different concurring opinions, struck down state efforts to collect taxes and fees designed to fund state efforts at monitoring and controlling migrants. These taxes were ruled to be against the federal powers of regulating maritime law and international shipping. The court failed to establish overall federal supremacy on the matter of immigration, however, and Justice Levi Woodbury emphasized the point in his dissenting opinion:

> [I]t is for the State where the power resides to decide on what is sufficient cause for it, whether municipal or economical, sickness

---

[6]Michael A. Schoeppner, *Moral Contagion: Black Atlantic Sailors, Citizenship, and Diplomacy in Antebellum America* (Cambridge, Mass.: Cambridge University Press, 2019), p. 106.

[7]*New York v. Miln*, 36 U.S. 11 Pet. 102 102 (1837), https://supreme.justia.com/cases/federal/us/36/102/.

[8]*Smith v. Turner; Norris v. Boston*, 48 U.S. (7 How.) 283 (1849).

or crime; as, for example, danger of pauperism, danger to health, danger to morals, danger to property, danger to public principles by revolutions and change of government, or danger to religion.[9]

Similarly, according to Neuman, Justice "Peter Daniel invoked at length the Jeffersonian polemics against the Alien Act of 1798 to demonstrate that power over the entry of aliens was vested exclusively in the states."[10,11]

These cases came in the wake of more notorious episodes during the 1820s and 1830s in southern states in which some states prohibited free black sailors from coming ashore in port cities. Fearing the presence of free blacks would incite slave uprisings, some southern states—but most vigorously South Carolina—essentially adopted "quarantine" laws in which free black sailors were required to stay on their ships or be held in the local jail until they departed again out of port.[12] Captains of British ships, which sometimes employed free blacks from British colonies, complained to federal authorities. Ultimately, however, the federal government was unwilling or unable to take steps that ended these policies.

Restricting State-to-State Migrants

The issue of race influenced other restrictions on migration as well. Some states, both north and south, adopted laws designed to restrict the movement of free blacks from state to state. Michelle Slack points out

---

[9]Gerald L. Neuman, *Strangers to the Constitution: Immigrants, Borders, and Fundamental Law* (Princeton, N.J.: Princeton University Press, 1996), p. 46.

[10]Neuman, "The Lost Century of American Immigration Law (1776–1875)," p. 1889.

[11]Some originalists have claimed that the passage of the Alien and Sedition Acts proves that the federal government has Constitutional authority over immigration. The Jeffersonians, of course, disagreed vehemently. The loss of the Federalists to the Republicans in 1800 essentially destroyed the pro-federal, anti-immigration position for decades, during which time federal immigration control was associated with the overreach of the Federalist Party, and contrary to the more strict Constitutional views of the Jeffersonians.

[12]Schoeppner, *Moral Contagion.*

the Oregon Constitution of 1857, although prohibiting slavery and involuntary servitude, also prohibited the entry or presence of any "negro or mulatto" not already residing in the State at the time of its adoption. Moreover, most free black residents were required to register and prove both their free status and their right to residence within the state. In turn, such documentation was regularly demanded of free blacks under threat of expulsion.[13]

The State of Illinois also imposed penalties for facilitating "entry by a mulatto."[14] In slave states, the situation was more focused on re-entry. Neuman writes:

> Slave state legislation usually barred the entry of free blacks who were not already residents of the state. Penalties were often imposed on persons bringing in free blacks. Over time, some states extended these prohibitions to their own free black residents who sought to return after traveling outside the state, either to a disapproved location or to any destination at all. Slave states often required that emancipated slaves leave the state forever, on pain of reenslavement.[15]

Although these laws were bound up with slavery and race, they nevertheless established both in the courts and in legislatures that states had the prerogative to prevent entry of certain persons into the states. Practical realities, of course, meant there was mostly free movement between states. As was also the case with the fugitive slave acts, limiting movement of Americans of any color, when it came to state-to-state travel, was exceptionally difficult in nineteenth-century America.[16]

---

[13] Michelle R. Slack, "Ignoring the Lessons of History: How the 'Open Borders' Myth Led to Repeated Patterns in State and Local Immigration Control," *Journal of Civil Rights and Economic Development* 27, no. 3 (Winter 2014): 474.

[14] Neuman, *Strangers to the Constitution,* p. 35.

[15] Ibid., p. 35.

[16] Although claiming to favor "states' rights," slave masters demanded greater federal action on the matter of fugitive slaves. Significantly, when South Carolina seceded from the Union, it cited insufficient federal action on the matter of returning fugitive slaves to bondage.

Congress Shows Little Interest
in Regulating Immigrants

Meanwhile, Congress largely ignored the immigration issue beyond regulating naturalization, as mandated in the Constitution. The 1911 report from Congress's Dillingham Commission on immigration recounts that legislation addressing immigration during the mid-nineteenth century was minimalist, to say the least. The commission notes that most agitation for new immigration legislation stemmed from the Native American Party, also known as the "Know-Nothings." These efforts failed due to a lack of interest by federal lawmakers in regulating immigration, and also due to doubts about whether or not such efforts were even constitutional. A lengthy quotation from the Commission's report helps illustrate the Congress's inaction on the matter:

> On January 2, 1855, Representative Wentworth, of Massachusetts, introduced a bill to prevent the introduction of foreign paupers, criminals, idiots, lunatics, and insane and blind persons, but it was laid on the table by a vote of 68 to 83...
>
> February 17, 1855, Senator Jones, of Tennessee, evidently believing it useless to try to pass an act excluding undesirables, sought to have Congress agree to give the matter entirely over to the States, and presented the following resolution, which was quickly tabled:
>
>> Whereas the Constitution of the United States confers on Congress the power to establish a uniform rule of naturalization and is silent as to the exercises of any power over the subject of immigration; and Whereas it is declared in the Constitution that all power not delegated to the constitution nor prohibited to the states by it are reserved to the States respectively or to the people:
>>
>> Therefore Resolved, that Congress has no power to pass any law regulating or controlling immigration into any of the States of Territories of the Union; but that the power to prescribe such rules and regulations touching this subject as may be deemed necessary to the safety and happiness of the people belongs to the States respectively or to the people, and that each State may determine for itself the evils resulting from the great influx of criminals

and paupers and apply such remedy as their wisdom may suggest for their safety demand.

Again on March 4, 1856, Mr. Smith, of Alabama, introduced a bill to exclude foreign paupers and criminals. This bill required United States consuls to issue certificates to all persons intending to come to the United States, stating that they were not paupers, nor convicts, and that they were coming of their own accord and were not sent out of their own country by any society or authority whatsoever...[17]

The bill failed to pass. Meanwhile, the Committee on Foreign Affairs issued a report on Congressional concerns about European nations dumping undesirables in the United States. But, the committee "seemed to doubt the power of Congress to regulate the matter, so almost all their recommendations were to the States..."[18] The lack of federal action on immigration matters led the Commission to conclude that it wasn't until the 1860s that "the change of control of immigration from the various States to the National Government" began to take place.[19]

The Federalization of Immigration Policy: The 1870s and After

As with so much else following the Civil War, what had been long accepted to be state policy began to be federalized, and in 1872, President Grant sent a message to Congress claiming that when it came to immigration, "I see no subject more national in its character..."

Hirota concurs with this assessment of latter-day federalization, noting that:

The federalization of immigration control was therefore a gradual process at best, and the actions of officials in the northeastern

---

[17]William P. Dillingham, "Reports of the Immigration Commission: Immigration Legislation, Document No. 758," December 5, 1910 (Washington, D.C.: Government Printing Office, 1911), p. 15.

[18]Ibid., p. 16.

[19]Ibid., p. 566.

states set the conditions for the introduction of general deportation by the federal government in 1891.

The nationalization of immigration regulation technically reached completion in 1891. Responding to the inefficiency of state-federal joint administration at [the New York immigration facility known as] Castle Garden revealed in legislative investigations, Congress passed a new immigration act in March 1891. The act placed issues of immigration under the control of the federal superintendent of immigration in the Treasury Department and appointed federal commissioners of immigration at major ports, replacing state enforcers with federal employees....The 1891 law also expanded the excludable category to cover people with mental defects and insanity, paupers and people "likely to become a public charge," people with contagious diseases, people convicted of a felony of other crime involving "moral turpitude, polygamists, and assisted emigrants"—making all of them deportable.[20]

The 1891 act came at the end of a decade of growing federal action on immigration which included the Chinese Exclusion Act and more general legislation soon afterward. By the time this was taking place, however, many state governments, especially those in Massachusetts and New York were inviting more federal involvement in immigration control. Hirota continues:

Officials in both New York and Massachusetts fundamentally influenced the development of national immigration policy in the late nineteenth century by playing a central role in the making of the federal Immigration Act of 1882. Passed three months after the enactment of the federal Chinese Exclusion Act of 1882, which suspended the immigration of Chinese laborers, the Immigration Act was the first general legislation that applied to all foreigners at a national level and set the groundwork for subsequent federal immigration laws....Modeled on existing immigration policies in New York and Massachusetts, these provisions came from a draft bill that the two states' officials created. In addition, the act left the enforcement of its provisions in the hands of the state officials.[21]

---

[20]Hirota, *Expelling the Poor*, p. 201.
[21]Ibid., p. 5.

Here we see that even in the 1880s, federal immigration laws continued to rely on local enforcement, and state and federal officials were seen as partners in regulation of migrants.

It would not be until the twentieth century that the federal government would begin to claim sole legal authority over matters of immigration.

That most of this legislative history is today forgotten would be an understatement. This led Neuman in 1993 to refer to a "myth of open borders" in which it has been long assumed, even by the very learned, that borders in the United States were essentially open with few to no attempts by governments at any level to control the flow of migrants either into the United States, or across state borders.

Slack notes that even among those who are aware of this legislative history, there have still been attempts to claim that no deportations of any consequence took place. As the work of Hirota has shown, this was not the case.

Efforts to Increase Immigration

Immigration policy cut both ways, however. Although some states sought to limit immigration, many other states sought to augment population growth by further encouraging foreign immigration. Many frontier states adopted policies designed to attract migrants by offering an easy road to citizenship, and by adopting multiple "official" languages designed to accommodate a non-English speaking population. Indeed, pro-immigrant sentiment mid-century was sufficient enough for President John Tyler to publicly declare in 1841: "We hold out to the people of other countries an invitation to come and settle among us as members of our rapidly growing family, and for the blessings which we offer them we require of them to look upon our country as their country and unite with us in the great task of preserving our institutions and thereby perpetuating our liberties."[22]

---

[22]Jonathan French, ed., *The True Republican* (Philadelphia, Penn.: James L. Gihon, 1854.), p. 249.

It must be understood, though, that by "people of other countries," Tyler did not mean all those categories of paupers and other undesirables outlined in state statutes. He meant people *other* than the disabled, ill, impoverished, and criminally inclined. Indeed, while Emma Lazarus was penning her famous poem "The New Colossus" in 1883—which claimed the US welcomed the world's "wretched refuse"—both the federal government and the states were at work enforcing legislation specifically designed to reject this alleged "refuse."

This effort to exclude undesirables, however, illustrates a fundamental difference between nineteenth-century immigration legislation and modern legislation. As Neuman observed "[n]either Congress nor the states attempted to impose *quantitative* limits on immigration" (emphasis in the original).[23]

Legislation focused instead on refusing entry to those who were seen as likely to increase the government-assistance rolls or who might commit criminal acts. Creating arbitrary quotas for the total number of legal immigrants was a later innovation.

Declarant Alien Voting

For one final illustration of the degree to which states controlled immigration policy within their borders is the example of so-called "declarant alien voting."

Although some states sought to expand regulations limiting immigration throughout much of the nineteenth century, numerous other state governments were extremely open to immigration, and immigrants. The drive to ease entry for immigrants was so widespread, that it led to situations in which new immigrants were able to obtain de facto citizenship with minimal fuss and paperwork by merely declaring an intent to become citizens.

Specifically, states that welcomed these "declarant" aliens as voters explicitly noted in their constitutions that non-US citizens were eligible to vote in elections if they declared their intent to become

---

[23]Gerald L. Neuman, *Strangers to the Constitution: Immigrants, Borders, and Fundamental Law* (Princeton, N.J.: Princeton University Press, 1996), p. 19.

citizens within a certain time frame before the election. In the case of Colorado, for example, the state's original 1876 constitution reads (Article VII section 1):

> [The voter] shall be a citizen of the United States, or not being a citizen of the United States, he shall have declared his intention, according to law, to become such citizen, not less than four months before he offers to vote.[24]

There was nothing innovative about this position, however. This standard for voting rights was simply continuing what was the status quo in Colorado since declarant alien voting rights had already been established years before within the Kansas Territory, out of which Colorado was eventually formed.

Declarant alien voting in state constitutions goes back at least to the Wisconsin constitution of 1848. By the mid-nineteenth century, it had spread to numerous Western territories via Congressional approval. And, as Neuman notes:

> Congress enfranchised declarant aliens in the [Oregon, Minnesota,] Washington, Kansas, Nebraska, Nevada, Dakota, Wyoming, and Oklahoma Territories. In all nine of these territories, Congress imposed the additional requirement of an oath to support the United States Constitution.
>
> Some, though not all, of the territories that permitted alien suffrage retained it when they achieved statehood. Older states joined the trend. When Indiana and Michigan adopted new constitutions in the early 1850s, they enfranchised declarant aliens. Reportedly, the change reflected competition for immigrants among the Midwestern states. Numerous former Confederate states adopted the same tactic, at least temporarily, after the civil war.[25]

Declarant alien voting eventually died out in the 1920s as new immigrants from Eastern and Southern Europe were deemed insufficiently "white" and the anti-immigration policies became more

---

[24]"The Constitution of the State of Colorado, Adopted in Convention, March 14, 1876" (Denver: Tribune Book and Job Printing House, 1876), p. 24, https://www.colorado.gov/pacific/sites/default/files/Colorado%20Constitution.pdf.
[25]Neuman, *Strangers to the Constitution*, p. 66.

popular for a variety of reasons. Anti-German hysteria during World War I, for example, was one cause.

In many states of the far west, however (such as Colorado) voting requirement had been very weak, even when there was a risk of non-whites voting. The 1876 Colorado constitution even stipulates that all new laws be published in English, Spanish, and German, so as to be intelligible to both Mexican-American and German-American immigrants.

Even Citizenship Became (Indirectly) a State Matter

Jamin Raskin, in "Legal Aliens, Local Citizens" finds that "white male aliens...exercised the right to vote in at least twenty-two states and territories during the nineteenth century."[26] In the nineteenth century, in a time of no income tax and few federal laws, citizenship was largely synonymous with voting rights.

Given the central role of state law in granting access to federal elections, states thus had the power to indirectly determine who could act as US citizens in terms of political participation:

> As a chapter in the history of American federalism, the period of alien suffrage reflected a conception of states as sovereign political entities. The states with alien suffrage allowed non-US citizens to participate in voting at all levels of American government, thereby turning them, explicitly or implicitly, into "citizens" of the state itself. Participant states were thus exercising independence from the national government for the purposes of communal political self-definition.[27]

The emergence of voting policies peculiar to certain states grew naturally out of the fact that during the nineteenth century, there was a distinction between citizenship in a particular state, and citizenship in the United States overall. In her book on the 1818 Illinois state Constitution, Ann Lousin notes virtually all adult white men could

---

[26]Jamin B. Raskin, "Legal Aliens, Local Citizens: The Historical Constitutional and Theoretical Meanings of Alien Suffrage," *University of Pennsylvania Law Review* 141, no. 4 (April 1993): 1397, https://digitalcommons.wcl.american.edu/facsch_lawrev/1044.

[27]Ibid., pp. 1397–98.

vote in the state at the time, and, "as was typical in early state constitutions, there was no requirement of United States citizenship."[28] In fact, by the late nineteenth century, there arose a legal phenomenon of multi-level citizenship that did not assume that all state citizens were also US citizens.

In Neuman's legal analysis, he finds that the state courts in several cases concluded that "alien voters were citizens of the state, though not of the United States."[29] Specifically, according to Neuman, the Wisconsin Supreme Court "described the independence of state citizenship from US citizenship as an acceptable consequence of the dual-sovereign system of federalism....A few other state courts similarly construed declarant alien voters as citizens of the state."[30] Essentially, the Wisconsin Supreme Court declared that "declarant aliens were citizens of Wisconsin" regardless of what the federal courts might say.

As voting was a central indicator of citizenship at the time, it should be noted that this followed logically from the fact that the states and not the central government were recognized as the proper instrument for regulating elections and voting rights. After all, in the text of the US constitution (ignoring later case law) it is clear that the states decide who is eligible to vote, and not the federal government. In fact, the federal constitution rarely mentions voting at all. According to Joshua Douglas, "unlike virtually every state constitution, the US constitution does not actually confer the right to vote on anyone."[31] There are only negative mandates as to who may *not* be disenfranchised. Even the US Supreme court admits this, and in 2013, the court's majority wrote: "Congress... regulate[s] *how* federal elections are held, but not *who* may vote in them. The latter is the province of the States."[32]

---

[28]Ann Lousin, *The Illinois State Constitution* (Oxford, U.K.: Oxford University Press, 2009), p. 5.

[29]Neuman, *Strangers to the Constitution*, p. 67.

[30]Ibid., p. 68.

[31]Joshua A. Douglas, "The Right to Vote Under State Constitutions," *Vanderbilt Law Review* 67, no. 1 (January 2014): 93.

[32]*Arizona, et al v. Inter Tribal Council of Arizona, Inc., et al.*, 677 F. 3d 383 (2013).

In state constitutions, voting and voting eligibility is a central topic, and this is a relic of nineteenth-century decentralist attitudes in which voting rights and thus citizenship (practically speaking) were well within the realm of the state legislatures.

Douglas goes on to note that frequent claims by federal courts that voting rights are "fundamental" to federal law cite no actual text in the US constitution, but appear to be based on nebulous philosophical claims. Only the state constitutions treat voting rights as fundamental. Historically, and in practical application, it has often been states and state constitutions that decide who can and who cannot exercise the prerogatives of a full citizen.

As with abortion, immigration policy in the United States has been federalized, in spite of immigration policy long being regarded as outside the prerogatives of federal policymakers. And, as with abortion, the federalization of immigration policy has led to a heightening of the political stakes of national elections, while also increasing tensions between blocs of voters from different states and regions who hold increasingly divergent views.

19

Why Indian Tribal Sovereignty Is Important

D uring much of 2016, construction of the Dakota Access Pipeline drew a number of lengthy protests stemming from concerns over the impact of the pipeline on the region's ground water. The pipeline also passed near the Standing Rock Indian Reservation which drew opposition from some members from the Sioux tribe and other tribes. Tribal governments became involved, and as a result, federal regulators became involved also.

In late 2016, in the midst of the protests, Donald Trump's transition team—during pre-inauguration preparations—suggested that it may pursue efforts to "privatize" Indian reservation lands as a means of streamlining the pipeline construction process.[1]

What would be the purpose of this "privatization"? According to several sources within the Trump transition team, the stated intent of the privatization policy was to allow tribal governments to circumvent US federal regulations in favor of more localized decision-making. According to Reuters:

---

[1] Valerie Volcovici, "Trump advisors aim to privatize oil-rich Indian reservations," *Reuters*, December 5, 2016, https://www.reuters.com/article/US-usa-trump-tribes-insight-idUSKBN13U1B1.

Now, a group of advisors to President-elect Donald Trump on Native American issues wants to free those resources from what they call a suffocating federal bureaucracy that holds title to 56 million acres of tribal lands, two chairmen of the coalition told Reuters in exclusive interviews...

The tribes have legal rights to use the land, but they do not own it. They can drill it and reap the profits, but only under regulations that are far more burdensome than those applied to private property.

"We should take tribal land away from public treatment," said Markwayne Mullin, a Republican US Representative from Oklahoma and a Cherokee tribe member who co-chaired Trump's Native American Affairs Coalition. "As long as we can do it without unintended consequences, I think we will have broad support around Indian country."[2]

The idea here was that many officials and residents within tribal lands and tribal governments wanted the pipeline to proceed, and this was more likely to happen if federal involvement could be minimized.

It was never quite clear what the Trump team meant by "privatization," but if privatization in this context meant taking more land out of the hands of the US federal government, then that's a good thing. On the other hand, if privatization meant the dissolution of Indian reservations and other tribal institutions, that would be a bad thing. Whether or not tribal governments are reformed or dissolved should, of course, be up to the people who live on tribal lands. But even for Americans who are not members of tribes and who do not live on tribal lands, tribal sovereignty has the potential to serve an important role in limiting federal power through political decentralization.

Tribal Lands Should Be Beyond the Reach of the Federal Government

The relationship between tribal governments and the US federal government has long been complex. To simplify greatly: the Indian

---

[2]Ibid.

tribes are sovereign governments, and their relationships with the US government are governed by bilateral treaties. In practice, however, the tribes are only semi-sovereign and are subject to federal oversight and federal regulation. The treaties that govern federal-tribal relations can be changed or disregarded unilaterally by the federal government. In practice, these "sovereign nations" have even less local control than the member states of the United States.

Nevertheless, the tribes remain *de jure* political entities outside the states in which they are located and thus have a direct legal relationship with the federal government. They are, in this way, intended to enjoy some degree of independence from *both* the federal government and the state governments.

In recent years, some progress has been made, at least in the area of expanding tribal sovereignty in relation to US member states. For example, in 2019, in the case of *Herrera v. Wyoming* (2019), the US Supreme court overturned the lower courts' findings that tribal rights (established in an 1868 treaty with the United States government) in Wyoming had ceased when Wyoming became a state in 1890. According to the case summary:

> In 2014, Wyoming charged petitioner Clayvin Herrera with off-season hunting in Bighorn National Forest and being an accessory to the same. The state trial court rejected Herrera's argument that he had a protected right to hunt in the forest pursuant to the 1868 Treaty, and a jury convicted him.[3]

The right to hunt was limited to "unoccupied" lands, and Herrera contended *both* that the National Forest lands in which he was hunting was unoccupied, *and* that he had a right to hunt there due to treaty stipulations. The court did not rule on whether or not the specific place Herrera was hunting was "occupied," but focused instead on whether or not tribal-members' rights continued to exist in accordance with an extant treaty. The court found these rights do still exist, but Herrera may still be found guilty if it is established the land on which he was hunting is not unoccupied.

---

[3] *Herrera v. Wyoming*, No. 17-532, 587 U.S. (2019), https://www.supremecourt.gov/opinions/18pdf/17-532_q86b.pdf.

Whether or not Herrera is ultimately found guilty, the court's findings are important because they potentially establish a higher standard of sovereignty for tribal governments than had been previously admitted by the courts.

After all, the basic premise of treaties between the tribes and US government—at least as communicated to the tribes themselves—was that the tribes were sovereign entities entering into treaties with another sovereign entity (i.e., the US government). Over time, the US government took advantage of the tribes' lack of de facto independence to reinterpret treaties as documents subject to unilateral amendment and abrogation by the US Congress. Even worse, state governments in the US began to assert their own authority over tribes, even though the tribes were not parties to any sort of agreement with the state governments.

In recent decades, however, courts have slowly begun to limit state jurisdiction over tribes with the effect of providing more autonomy to tribes. Perhaps most famous among these decisions is the 1987 case *California v. Cabazon Band of Mission Indians* in which the court determined state governments could not prevent tribes from offering legal gambling within their own borders (in most cases). The result was political decentralization and greater access to legal gambling for non-tribal members. The subsequent rise of the gaming industry on tribal lands has greatly improved the standard of living for many Indians.

In *Herrera v. Wyoming*, the court further established that state governments cannot simply override treaty-established tribal law whenever it suits state legislatures. But this isn't the only case in recent years which has strengthened tribal independence. In March 2019, the Supreme Court decided in favor of the Yakama tribe in *Washington State Dept. of Licensing v. Cougar Den, Inc.* The Court held that the Yakama Nation Treaty of 1855 preempts state attempts to tax fuel purchased by a tribal corporation for sale to tribal members. The State of Washington insisted it could tax tribal fuel transported on state highways. The Supreme Court disagreed and took a relatively broad interpretation of the treaty's provisions guaranteeing use of the state's highways.

Decentralization
and Local Sovereignty Matters

These two cases, of course, are just very small steps in the right direction. For the most part, Congress can still abrogate and amend treaties on its own with precious little input from the tribes themselves. These recent cases help to establish greater tribal sovereignty in the face of state law, but do little—on their own—to enhance tribal sovereignty when it comes to federal legislation. Some observers might wrongly interpret these decisions as attacks on state-level sovereignty by lessening state control over its own territory. This, however, misses the point.

Correctly imagined, *both* state governments *and* tribal governments ought to have far greater independence both from federal control, and from each other. In practice, for example, the entire northeast corner of Arizona, which is mostly Navajo tribal land, ought not be considered Arizona territory at all. Nor should it be considered US territory.

For now, though, the federal government continues to exercise immense amounts of direct regulatory power over tribal lands, and can regulate internal tribal affairs right down to whether or not the tribes can legalize marijuana.

Nevertheless, the treaty-granted status of the tribes does constitute a check on the power of the federal government. This idea has been explored by Kevin Bourgault of the Center for Indigenous Self-Determination Research. Bourgault writes:

> Tribes are the sole entities in our society with established treaty rights....As sovereign nations, tribes are equivalent political entities to the states in which they are located.
>
> Tribes also are among the few entities that have an immediate claim to legal redress and mitigation. This means that tribes are uniquely positioned to act quickly within a legal system that is becoming more and more byzantine and unresponsive to immediate needs....[4]

---

[4]Kevin Bourgault, "Tribal power and important check on ruling elite," *The Register-Guard*, September 19, 2016, http://web.archive.org/web/20200713152505/

Bourgault has framed the argument in terms of environmental issues, but the larger issue here is one of decentralization. Since tribal governments are—at least theoretically—sovereign governments and arguably peers of the US government, they could potentially act as true obstacles to federal power, possibly to a greater extent than the governments of US member states. Whether or not this can be done in practice will depend on political realities.

But Tribal Governments Are Corrupt!

Unfortunately, the concept of tribal sovereignty continues to encounter opposition, often due to outsiders' concerns over political corruption within tribal governments. Some critics have (correctly) pointed out that tribal governments are often corrupt, with tribal officials using their privileges to enrich themselves at the expense of other tribal members. This corruption we are told, is sufficient grounds for the federal government to dissolve those governments and reform them as federal officials see fit.[5]

The call for dissolving tribal governments as a means of fighting corruption, however, is just as problematic as the claim that corruption at the state or local level of government is sufficient grounds for the federal government to dissolve those governments. Clearly, this would be a disastrous policy that would enormously expand federal power.

The proper position, of course, is to recognize that any efforts to make tribal governments less corrupt is a matter for tribal members and residents of tribal lands. Just as the residents of Texas should decide for themselves how the government of Texas works, so should the members of the Navajo Nation decide how the Navajo tribal government works. Federal involvement is simply

http://registerguard.com/rg/opinion/34780967-78/tribal-power-an-important-check-on-ruling-elite.html.csp.
[5]Carl Horowitz, "No Reservations: The Case for Dismantling the Indian Bureaucracy," *Townhall*, February 4, 2011, http://townhall.com/columnists/carlhorowitz/2011/02/04/no_reservations__the_case_for_dismantling_the_indian_bureaucracy.

not necessary. Non-Indians who do not wish to be subject to tribal government need not live on tribal lands or travel through them.

Indeed, the idea that the federal government will solve the problem of corruption in tribal government is thoroughly unconvincing given that corruption of tribal governments has long been largely a *product* of federal involvement in tribal affairs. Historically, federal officials are notorious for running their own puppet candidates in tribal elections who can serve as a direct conduit between tribal governments and the federal government's favored interest groups.

The Effects of Ignoring Tribal Sovereignty

The federal government's tribal policies have long functioned primarily to benefit the federal government itself. For example, since 1880, much of the land that has been removed from sovereign tribal hands has simply been added to the hundreds of millions of acres of federally owned lands. Experience suggests abolishing the tribes or their treaties would only convert tribal land into federal land, to be held by federal government agencies in perpetuity. The federal government already owns 640 million acres, and further expanding federal power over vast areas of land would only further enhance and centralize political institutions in the United States.

After all, lest we think that the feds can be trusted to privatize those lands or grant them to the states, we'd do well to remember that the reason the federal government presently owns so much land in the first place is because the federal government has repeatedly failed to follow through on promises to localize or privatize federal lands.[6]

Most of Western Colorado, for example, was Ute tribal land until 1880. When federal agencies seized that land from the tribe, only a portion was privatized or even transferred to states and local governments. Instead, most of that land today remains in federal hands.

---

[6]Ryan McMaken, "How the Feds Botched the Frontier Homestead Acts," *Mises Wire*, October 19, 2016, https://mises.org/blog/how-feds-botched-frontier-homestead-acts.

The sovereignty of locally-controlled tribal lands should be a priority, and be seen as a key factor in developing meaningful checks on federal power through local sovereignty and secession.

20

Sovereignty for Cities and Counties: Decentralizing the American States

I n 2021, during the era of covid-19 lockdowns and mask mandates, Florida governor Ron DeSantis signed new legislation largely banning the use of vaccine mandates by both private entities or local governments. The new legislation also reinforced the DeSantis administration's overall efforts to prevent local governments from imposing covid mask mandates. Most notably, the administration has intervened to prevent school districts from imposing mandates.

This approach predictably raised opposition. Generally, opponents of DeSantis's efforts at preempting local mandates claimed that local governments ought to exercise some degree of independence from state policies.

Days later, when pressed on this issue at a press conference, DeSantis responded with a philosophical statement suggesting that the prerogatives of state governments ought to trump all other levels of government. Specifically, when asked why he was willing to impose state mandates on local governments—i.e., "violating the tenet of home rule"—DeSantis responded:

> It's the United States of America, not the United school boards or county commissions of America. So the states are the primary vehicles to protect people's freedoms, their health, their safety, their welfare in our constitutional system.[1]

He goes on to emphasize that local governments must be at the mercy of his state-level administration because local governments "don't have the right to do wrong." What is "wrong," of course, is to be decided by state-level politicians. This response strongly implies that DeSantis is of the opinion Florida—and apparently all the other states as well—are to function as *unitary* states. That is, his position appears to be that decentralized power is appropriate in relations between state governments and the federal governments— but has no role in the relationship between state governments and local governments.

This debate raises an important issue that extends far beyond Florida's current debate over vaccine mandates.

Unitary States versus Confederations

Essentially, the question—at least for Americans—comes down to whether or not a decentralist ideal should be applied only to relations between state governments and the federal government. If this applies only to state-federal relations, then decentralization apparently ought to stop at state borders. Thus, were there to be formal or de facto secession of a state in the future, then that state would thereafter function as a sovereign unitary state. Current examples of unitary states include France and Perú, in which the central government exercises broad and supreme power over any administrative subdivisions such as municipalities, counties, or provinces. Moreover, these local entities are *creatures of the central government* in that

---

[1]"Florida Governor Ron DeSantis Press Conference Transcript November 18: Bans Vaccine Mandates," November 18, 2021. https://www.rev.com/blog/transcripts/florida-governor-ron-desantis-press-conference-transcript-november-18-bans-vaccine-mandates

the central government governs them directly and can even abolish local governments without local consent.

Most countries in the world employ unitary governments. Moreover, the member states of the US themselves are currently unitary in nature. Municipalities and counties are creations of state law, and city and county governments can be created or abolished by acts of the state legislature. In some states, local governments enjoy some degree of autonomy through "home rule" provisions or statutes, but even in these cases, political power lies lopsidedly with the state government.

This is in contrast with the state-federal relationship in the US. Although the US states' power relative to the federal government has been thoroughly weakened in recent decades, it is still clear that the US government must frequently rely on financial incentives to get what they want from state governments, rather than imposing policies directly. Indeed, the covid crisis has highlighted the limits of federal powers within states in that—unlike in unitary states—the national government clearly never had the legal power to impose nationwide "lockdowns."

On the other hand, because of the *states'* unitary structures, state governors—unlike the US president—have wielded immense power directly over lower levels of government. In the case of state governors, this means he or she can exercise direct authority over municipal and county governments, imposing lockdowns, mask mandates, and more.

So the question remains: when US member states begin to obtain greater autonomy from the US federal government—which is inevitable either in the near future or the more distant future—will this simply lead to the creation of new unitary states exercising centralized political power over their own populations?

It would seem that any principled defense of decentralization must lead to calls for decentralization *at the state level as well.*

After all, to support a de facto or de jure independent and unitary state in say, Florida, would be simply to embrace the dominant European model.

Moreover, elections in one of these new unitary American regimes would become exactly what defenders of the electoral college have sought to avoid: statewide elections would—and presently *do*—reflect nothing more than majoritarianism, with the executive chosen based on the principle of winning 50 percent of the votes plus one. There would be no mechanism to balance regional political realities as the electoral college does with presidential elections now.

How to Turn US States into Confederations

If decentralization is something we take seriously—and not just a temporary ploy to get more autonomy for certain state governments—then state governments themselves must be limited by local autonomy.

Specifically, governance in these places must be subjected to tools that protect local autonomy. These tools include double majorities, local vetoes, and political representation not based on population size.

For example, let's look at a state like Colorado. Were the state to become an independent unitary state, the Denver metro area would exercise almost untrammeled power over the rest of the state. The western half of the state and the metro areas outside of Denver would be at the mercy of Denver-area voters. This, of course, is *currently* the situation in terms of statewide policy.

The answer to this could be found in giving metropolitan areas outside Denver a way to veto statewide policies that benefit only one or two regions of the state at the expense of everyone else. For example, a system of double majorities could be employed. This would mean that significant legislative changes would need to be approved by both a majority of the voters overall and also by a majority of voters in a majority of regional governments. (This system is presently used in Switzerland.) Similarly, different regions of the state would need to be given equal votes within a legislative body. That way each region of the state would be on equal footing regardless of each region's population. This would prevent the highly populated regions from riding roughshod over more rural regions. Moreover, supermajorities in the style of the old Articles of Confederation ought to be required.

Without measures such as these, these unitary governments would be governed on no principle other than rank majoritarianism.

But perhaps most importantly of all, it must be explicit that the state's municipalities or regional governments can legally secede. Without this guarantee, we'd simply be looking at an eventual repeat of what we see now in the United States: an entrenched ruling class at the national capital exercising outsized power to force policy on all regions of the nation regardless of local values, laws, or preferences.

So, DeSantis's view that state governments are necessarily the "primary vehicles" through which policy ought to be made is a dangerous view. It appears to presuppose that there is something magical about the state level of government and that no further decentralization of power is necessary.

DeSantis is, of course, correct that federal attempts to impose national covid mandates are dangerous and illegitimate. But he is wrong that decentralization is necessary only in limiting *federal* power. The danger of state-level power is especially present for larger states like Florida, California, New York, and Texas. These states have populations the size of medium-sized European countries, and thus already consolidate far too much power into a small handful of unitary regimes. We could contrast states like Texas, for example—with 25 million people governed under a unitary regime—with a decentralized confederation like Switzerland, with 8 million people spread over twenty-six mostly self-governing cantons. Most of these cantons have populations of less than 1 million. It might strike some secessionists as fine to centralize political power in Sacramento or Austin or Tallahassee so long as these polities have escaped the federal boot. But this scheme will only set up an eventual repeat of the sorts of federal abuses we see today.

Postscript
A Tale of Two Megastates:
Why the EU Is Better
(In Some Ways) than the US

Over the years, I've been pretty hard on the European Union. Both as an editor and a writer, I've published articles criticizing its central bank and its unelected, bureaucratic central government. Especially objectionable is the EU ruling class's propensity for cynical politics built around threatening and intimidating voters and national governments who don't conform to Brussels' wishes.

Recall, for example, how the EU threatened[1] the United Kingdom with retaliatory tariffs to dissuade the British from voting to pull the UK out of the EU.[2] Many within the EU continue to

---

[1]James Crisp, "EU mulls carbon tariffs in climate trade war warning shot to Brexit Britain," *The Telegraph*, February 8, 2020, https://www.telegraph.co.uk/business/2020/02/08/eu-mulls-carbon-tariffs-climate-trade-war-warning-shot-brexit/+&cd=2&hl=en&ct=clnk&gl=us.

[2]Jamie Dettmer, "EU Threatens Retaliations, Tariffs in Northern Ireland Dispute with Britain," *VOANews*, March 5, 2021, https://www.voanews.

push petty anti-British policies to this day.[3] Moreover, the Brussels government has taken steps to force into line various EU member states that don't conform to EU edicts on immigration or internal politics.

For example, over the past year, Brussels has launched legal proceedings against Poland because of steps taken by Poland's elected government to reform the regime's judicial system.[4] The EU has also taken legal action against Poland, Hungary, and the Czech Republic over immigration policy.[5] Even worse, many within the bloc continue to push for a so-called United States of Europe, which will presumably drive the bloc toward far more political unity and control by the Brussels regime.[6]

Simply put, the EU is a force for political centralization which threatens to further abolish what remains of more localized autonomy in Europe.

EU Centralization Is Bad, the United States Is Even Worse

Yet, for all of the EU's insistence on moving in the wrong direction—that is, the direction of political centralization—the EU remains remarkably decentralized by American standards. Indeed, when it comes to its degree of centralization, and the degree to

---

com/europe/eu-threatens-retaliations-tariffs-northern-ireland-dispute-britain.
[3]Jonathan Miller, "Why doesn't Emmanuel Macron like Britain?," *The Spectator*, January 24, 2019, https://www.spectator.co.uk/article/why-doesn-t-emmanuel-macron-like-britain-.
[4]"EU steps up legal action against Poland over courts' independence," *Reuters*, January 27, 2021, https://finance.yahoo.com/news/eu-steps-legal-action-against-130339874.html.
[5]Gabriela Baczynska, "EU to open case against Poland, Hungary, Czech Republic over migration," *Reuters*, https://www.reuters.com/article/us-europe-migrants-eu-infringements-idUSKBN1931O4.
[6]Judith Mischke, "Germans, French most in favor of a 'United States of Europe,' poll," *Politico*, December 28, 2017, https://www.politico.eu/article/united-states-of-europe-germans-french-most-in-favor-poll/.

which the central bureaucracy exercises control over member states, the EU is far less centralized than the United States.

This is evident in several ways. When it comes to border control, welfare programs, and control over each member state's political institutions, the EU clearly tolerates more local control than is the case in the United States. Best of all, it is still possible for EU member states to actually leave the union, as demonstrated by Brexit.

Indeed, for those of us who favor greater political decentralization in the United States, a step toward the EU's current situation would be a move in the right direction for the US—at least in terms of its political structure—even if the EU itself is presently trending in the wrong direction.

The European Welfare State Is More Decentralized

One key area in which Europe is more decentralized than the US is its welfare state. European member states are fortunate in that their welfare programs remain decentralized, and that the bloc does not have any social benefits program comparable to the US's Social Security program.

This isn't to say the EU doesn't have any social-spending programs administered in Brussels. The EU bureaucracy takes in tax revenues from member states and then redistributes those funds around the bloc. In practice, this means wealthier EU members are net payers while poorer EU members are net receivers. Funds largely go toward "economic development" projects and agriculture.[7]

Although transfer payments are a reality in the EU, the EU has nothing like the US's system of a single nationwide program that directly taxes individuals and then pays that money back out directly to individuals.

For example, with Social Security and Medicare, individual workers in the US are *directly* taxed by the central government and then those funds are transferred by the central government from

---

[7]Tamara Kovacevic, "EU budget: Who pays most in and who gets most back?," *BBC News*, May 28, 2019.

wage earners to retirees. Other similar programs include food stamps and Medicaid.

This means millions of Americans look directly to the federal government for a "check in the mail." Although all US states have their own welfare programs of various sorts, these tend to be very small compared to the federal welfare apparatus. Naturally, this tends to give the federal government far more control over the lives and personal budgets of Americans than if the welfare system were funded and administered at the state or municipal level.[8]

In Europe, by contrast, the welfare state is administered and funded overwhelmingly at the level of the member country. Britain's National Health Service has always been a *British* program. The same is true of the UK's pension programs.

Other member states function in a similar fashion. France, for example, has an immense welfare state, but those who receive transfer payments through the French system do not ultimately depend on the Brussels government for these payments.

The political implications of this are immense. The national nature of the American welfare state acts as an enormous impediment to any effort of an American state to break away from the union. Any American state that seeks to leave the US would, for instance, likely face opposition from voters who fear the loss of benefits—especially Social Security—doled out by the central government. Indeed, were the European welfare state unified to the degree that it is in the United States, it is extremely unlikely that Brexit would have ever happened. British pensioners and recipients of "EU welfare" payments would have been too fearful of losing their benefits—just as many opponents of Scotland's independent referendum

---

[8]Ryan McMaken, "Decentralize the Welfare State," *Mises Wire*, May 25, 2017, https://mises.org/wire/decentralize-welfare-state. When we look at GDP and per capita GDP, we find most US states have larger and more robust economies than most European welfare states. For example, even the poorest US states like Mississippi and West Virginia have economies large enough to fund welfare states similar to those which already exist in many areas of southern and eastern Europe. Numerous European examples have already shown that when it comes to welfare states, bigness is not necessary.

feared the loss of transfer payments from London. It's not a coincidence that elderly residents of Scotland (and "out-of-work benefits claimants") lopsidedly voted against Scottish independence.[9]

The Member States' Legislatures Still Dominate Lawmaking in the Bloc

Government regulation in Europe is increasingly a matter for politicians in Brussels. Yet, for the most part, the administration of government continues to be dominated by the governments of the member states.

Although the tug-of-war between Brussels and the national legislatures continues,[10] the fact is member states generally retain unilateral control over national budgets, law-and-order issues, and over social policies like abortion.[11] There is no European equivalent of the FBI, for instance.[12]

As conflicts within the bloc between east and west over migrants continues, we see that member states are both more willing and more

---

[9]Steven Ayres, "Demographic differences and voting patterns in Scotland's independence referendum," House of Commons Library, September 23, 2014, https://commonslibrary.parliament.uk/demographic-differences-and-voting-patterns-in-scotlands-independence-referendum/.

[10]Viraj Bhide, "Germany Pushes Back against the ECB's Bailouts," *Mises Wire*, May 13, 2020, https://mises.org/wire/germany-pushes-back-against-ecbs-bailouts.

[11]Antonia Mortenson, "Poland puts new restrictions on abortion into effect, resulting in a near-total ban on terminations," *CNN News*, January 28, 2021, https://www.cnn.com/2021/01/28/europe/poland-abortion-restrictions-law-intl-hnk/index.html.

[12]Ryan McMaken, "Dismantle the FBI, and give its Money Back to the States," *Mises Wire*, May 12, 2017, https://mises.org/wire/dismantle-fbi-and-give-its-money-back-states. While the US's federal government has created a number of nationwide police forces (i.e., the Federal Bureau of Investigation) the European experience has made it clear that a large unified police force of this type is not necessary. Europe relies primarily on Interpol, a far more decentralized model for policing which relies on local control. Interpol agents, for example, do not have police powers, and do not have the power to make arrests.

capable of pushing back against edicts from the central government than is the case with American states.[13]

Member states even have unilateral control over their own national borders. While most members of the EU are subject, de jure, to the Schengen Agreement and its successor agreements, member states still maintain de facto unilateral control. This was on clear display during the early months of the covid-19 panic, when numerous member states within the EU closed down much of the travel across their borders.[14]

Exit Is Still Possible

Nothing better illustrates the EU's greater level of decentralization than the fact that member states can still peacefully and legally leave the bloc. This was demonstrated when the United Kingdom finally left the EU after several years of negotiations following the national referendum on Brexit in 2016. Although the Brussels government sought to make it as difficult as possible for the UK to withdraw, it was nonetheless impossible to deny that the UK could legally do so. Moreover, in the practical sense, there was ultimately nothing the EU could do to prevent the UK from leaving, largely because the other EU members were not willing to support military action to force the UK to continue within the bloc.

We could, of course, contrast this with the United States. In the case of the US, anytime Americans hint at the possibility of secession, opponents of secession chortle that "the secession question was solved by the US Civil War!" Those who invoke this phrase, of course, are signaling that they believe any attempt at secession justifies military invasion and occupation of separatist territories.

---

[13]Jonas Ekblom, "Poland, Hungary broke EU laws by refusing to host migrants: court adviser," *Reuters*, October 31, 2019, https://www.reuters.com/article/us-europe-migration-court-idUSKBN1XA1S5.

[14]"Border controls in Schengen due to coronavirus: what can the EU do?," The European Parliament, accessed June 22, 2020, https://www.europarl.europa.eu/news/en/headlines/security/20200506STO78514/reopeningschengen-borders-after-covid-19-what-can-eu-do.

Fortunately for the Europeans, the EU has yet to progress to the point where it can take military action against its own people with impunity. In America, on the other hand, any overture toward asserting independence from Washington brings veiled or not-so-veiled threats of violence.[15]

What Brussels Bureaucrats Really Want

None of this is to say that the bureaucrats who run the EU in Brussels wouldn't love to have all of the powers the US government currently enjoys. For years, the EU has been moving toward expanding its military capabilities, while calling for greater fiscal controls to expand the European Central Bank's monetary policy. Some now call for using the covid-19 crisis as a justification for creating a "stronger EU." But, however strong Europhiles' calls are for political unity, old habits die hard. Many Europeans still aren't willing to turn their national legislatures into mere adjuncts of a central government that will rule from Brussels.

On the other hand, Americans over the past century have had no such qualms about empowering a central state to a level that would delight any Europhile bureaucrat. It's too late for American member states to assert independence from the central government without facing an avalanche of legal, political, and even military opposition. Europeans would be wise to not put themselves in a similar position.

---

[15]Becket Adams, "That time Eric Swalwell threatened to go nuclear on gun owners. Literally," *Washington Examiner*, July 8, 2019, https://www.washingtonexaminer.com/opinion/that-time-eric-swalwell-threatened-to-go-nuclear-on-gun-owners-literally.

Index

Compiled by Roger E. Bissell

Abortion, 153, 173–9, 195, 215.
See also Roe vs. Wade
Anti-abortion, 173, 177–8
Centralization of abortion
policy, 178–9, 195
Pro-abortion, 178
Africa, 67n10, 70, 80, 83–84, 88,
97
Sub-Saharan Africa, 15
Aggregate wealth measures, 112
"agree to disagree," 179
Alabama, 109, 118, 166n10, 188
Alaska, 118, 178
Alesina, Alberto, 92
Algeria, 87
Alien Act of 1798, 185
Allison, Graham, 129n14
American Civil War, see United
States: Civil War
American Medical Association,
176
American Revolution, 75, 84, 162
American revolutionaries, 17,
60

Americas, the, 15, 41, 44. See also
Latin America; North America;
South America
Amsterdam (Netherlands), 7
Animal rights, 152–3
Anti-Federalists, 164
Anti-German hysteria, 193
Arcadia (California, US), 30
Arendt, Hannah, 49–51
Argentina, 88, 109
Arizona, 102, 118, 201
Arkansas, 118, 166n10
Armed neutrality as "disunion
completed" and "treason in
effect," 169
Articles of Confederation, 182.
See also United States Constitu-
tion
Asia, 16, 37, 39, 80, 83, 88, 91,
109, 128. See also United States
of East Asia
Asian colonies, 84, 88
East Asia, eastern Asia, 145
Southeast Asia, 115
Autonomy and diversity, 8

Australia, 48, 109
  Australian Senate, 142
Austria, 79–80, 119, 156
  Austria-Hungary, 16
  Austrian Republic, 80
Austrian economics, 4
Avignon, 78

Baechler, Jean, 38*n*4, 69
Bairoch, Paul, 116, 119
"balkanization," 80
Ball, Desmond, 135
Baltic states, 43, 49, 65, 67*n*10, 71,
  80
  Baltic-state nationalists, 72
  Basque Country, 84
Bassani, Luigi, 34, 34*n*6
Bastiat, Frederick, 8
Becker, Gary, 92, 95
Beckley-Bairoch approach, 119
Beckley, Michael, 113–17, 119,
  121
Belarus, 128
Belgium, 79, 108. *See also* Low
  Countries
  Belgian Communes, 78
Belgrade (Yugoslavia), 70
Berlin (Germany), 22
Biafra, 64, 70
Bilateral treaties, 199
Blue States of America, 118, 121
Bootle, Roger, 106
Borders, 8, 16-17, 30–34, 51, 68,
  75, 86, 107, 119, 121, 128–9,
  157, 190–1, 200, 206, 216
Borland, Elizabeth, 86–88
Bosnia-Herzegovina, 74. *See also*
  Yugoslavia

Bourgault, Kevin, 201–2
Brexit, 60, 89, 105, 213–14, 216
British state, fully independent
  and separate, 17, 47, 47*n*9, 48,
  121. *See also* England; United
  Kingdom
  British Empire, 17, 59
  British Parliament, 85, 121*n*13
  British voters, 17
Brodie, Janet Farrell, 174
Bryan, William Jennings, 60*n*16
Buckley, F.H., 96–97
Budapest, 73
  Budapest Memorandum, 130
Bush administration, 72

California, 30, 99–103, 109, 118,
  144, 171, 179, 183, 200
  Six Californias initiative, 102
*California v. Cabazon Band of
  Mission Indians*, 200
Canada, 48, 64–65, 88, 109, 120–
  1, 121*n*13, 131, 142, 167, 183
  Senate of Canada, 142
Caribbean, 41, 95
Carinthia, 80
Castello, Sergio, 91
Castle Garden, 189
Catalonian secessionists, 18
Catholic, 19*n*2, 143–4. *See also*
  Christian; Protestant
Center for Indigenous Self-Deter-
  mination Research, 201
Center for Nonproliferation Stud-
  ies, 127
Central Intelligence Agency, 115
Chechnya, 84
Chicago, 29, 29*n*3

China, 8, 15, 36–38, 49–50, 70,
    84, 111–12, 114–15, 117, 117n8,
    n10, 118–22, 130–1, 145
Chinese Exclusion Act, 189
Chittenden, Martin, 167
Chiu Yu Ko, 36n2
Christian, 101, 152. *See also*
    Catholic; Protestant
"Christian duty," 178
Circumcision, 86, 151–3
Citizenship, 190–1, 193–5
Classical liberal, Classical liberal-
    ism, 7, 54n2, 68, 162. *See also*
    Libertarian, Libertarianism
Cleveland (Ohio, US), 113
Clinton, Hillary, 153
Cobden, Richard, 8
Cold War, 51, 70, 115, 121. *See*
    also Iron Curtain
Colombia, 33
Colorado, 32, 109, 118, 132, 178,
    192–3, 203, 208
    1876 state constitution, 192–3
    Western Colorado, 203
Committee on Foreign Affairs,
    188
Composite Index of National
    Capability, 112, 114
Comstock Laws, 198
Connecticut, 118, 167–8
Constant, Benjamin, 8, 58–59, 61
Constitution, 7, 146. *See also* state
    constitution; United States:
    Constitution
Correlates of War Project, 117
Cunliffe, Marcus, 163
Cultural dialogue, 7
Cyprus, 64

Czechoslovakia, 65, 72–73
Czech Republic, 212

Dakota Access Pipeline, 197
Daniel, Peter, 185
Decentralization, 12–13, 15–19,
    19n2, 20, 32, 36, 39–40, 40n9,
    41, 41n10, 43, 59–61, 63, 66–68,
    77, 103, 124, 127, 141, 148, 198,
    200, 202, 207–8. *See also* seces-
    sion
    decentralization at the state
        level, 207
    internal decentralization, 16
"declarant" aliens, 191–2, 194
"decolonization," 67, 80, 83–85, 87
De facto independence, 15
Deist, Jeff, 13
Delaware, 118
Democratic government institu-
    tions, 12
"democratic ideal," 72
Democratic Party, 60
Democratic Republic of Geneva,
    147
Democratic Republic of the
    Congo, 64
de Molinari, Gustave, 58. 63
Denmark, 47, 48n10, 79–80, 97,
    106, 108–9
    Faroe Islands, 80
DeSantis, Ron, 205–6, 209
de Tocqueville, Alexis, 54
Dillingham Commission, 187
Direct taxation of individuals, 213
"Disposable surplus," 114
District of Columbia, 118
Dixon, Archibald, 169

Douglas, Joshua, 194

Easterly, William, 93, 96–97
East Timor, 44
Economic autarky, 90
Economic prosperity, 11, 18, 39,
    69, 145
Economic integration, 90–92
Economic self-sufficiency, 90
Efforts to limit prerogatives of
    powerful states, 12, 50, 56, 115
England, 38, 148. *See also* British
    state; United Kingdom
    English Civil war, 162
    English poor laws, 182
Entente powers, 80
Estonia, 70, 74, 81
Eurasia, 36n2, 128
Europe, 15, 19n2, 20, 34–38, 38n4,
    39–40, 40–41n9, 41–42, 43n1,
    44, 49–50, 53, 55, 60, 67n10,
    69–69, 77–78, 80, 83, 93–94, 96,
    99, 107–9, 115, 119, 121, 155,
    188, 207, 209, 212–14, 214n8,
    215, 215n12, 217. *See also* Latin
    Christendom; United States of
    Europe
    Central Europe, 73, 156
    Eastern Europe, 131, 156, 192,
        214n8
    European Central Bank, 217
    European colonial powers, 17
    European Commission (in
        Brussels), 17
    "European miracle," 36
    European unification, 8
    European Union, 17, 32, 34,
        41, 95, 211
    Europhile, 217

Northern Europe, 96, 107
Southeastern Europe, 120
Southern Europe, 192, 214n8
Western Europe, 40n9, 108,
    121

FBI, 215
Federalism, 18, 19n2, 146, 148,
    194
    Federalists, 163–4, 185n11
    "federally organized militia sys-
        tem," 165
Finland, 96, 106, 109
First World War, 47n9, 114, 161
Florida, 109, 118, 148, 166n10,
    205–6, 206n1, 207, 209
Food stamps, 214
Fowler, William Chauncey, 168
Foxley, Rachel, 162
France, 8, 39, 54–55, 67n10, 79,
    87, 90n1, 106, 108, 115, 121,
    130, 146–8, 206, 214
    French Enlightenment, 146
    French liberals, 54, 59
    French Republic, 59, 147
    French Revolution, 67n10, 78,
        146, 146n2, 147
Franklin, Benjamin, 9
Freedom, 9, 11, 18, 20, 23, 31–33,
    34n6, 38–39, 64–66, 68–70,
    101, 104, 148, 168, 206. *See also*
    liberty
Free market, 7, 66. *See also* Trade:
    Free trade
Friedman, Leon, 164

Gambling, Gaming industry, 200
"general will," 146–8

Genevan democracy, 147
Georgia, 118, 132
Germany, 49–50, 70, 80, 90*n*1,
    114–15, 119, 121, 152. *See also*
    East Germany, West Germany.
    East Germany, 32
    East Prussia, 80
    German-American immi-
        grants, 193
    German cities, 37
    German Confederation, 79
    "German Town Law," 156
    West Germany, 32
    Westphalian state, 44
Gerson, Michael, 134
Global federation, 8
Global polity and regime, 16
Gorbachev, Mikhail, 48*n*11
Grant, Ulysses S., 188
Great Britain, 79. *See also* United
    Kingdom
Greece, 28, 79, 106
    Greek Cyprus, 64
    Greek-Persian wars, 9
    Ionian Islands, 79, 81
Gross domestic product (GDP),
    95–96, 106, 109, 111–12,
    114–17, 117*n*8, *n*10, 118–19,
    121, 132, 135–6, 214*n*8
Guttmacher Institute, 175

Hawaii, 87, 118, 178
Hanseatic League, 107
Harrison, Lowell, 169
Haskell, P.S., 174
Hayek, F.A., 38*n*4
Headscarves, head coverings,
    152–153

Hechter, Michael, 86–88
Hegel, G.W.F., 9
Henry, Patrick, 164–5
Herrera, Clayvin, 199
Herrera v. Wyoming, 199–200
Higgs, Robert, 46
Hirota, Hidetaka, 182–4, 188–90
Hitler, Adolph, 22
Hobbes, Thomas, 8
Holy Roman Empire, 16
Hülsmann, Jörg Guido, 54*n*2
Human rights, 18–19, 22, 31, 54,
    59, 63, 151
Hungary, 49, 71, 94, 106, 212. *See
    also* Austria-Hungary

Iceland, 47, 48*n*10, 67*n*10, 79–81,
    93, 106, 151–2
Idaho, 118, 166*n*10
Illinois, 118, 166*n*10, 174–5, 177,
    186
    1818 state constitution, 193
Immigration policy, 181, 183,
    189–91, 195, 212
Imperialism, 75
India, 15, 36, 48, 50, 85, 112,
    119–20, 125, 203
    Indians (Asian), 85. *See also*
        Indians (Native American)
Indiana, 118, 166*n*10, 192
Indians (Native American),
    197–8, 200, 203. *See also* Indians
    (Asian)
    Navajo Nation, 202
    Standing Rock Indian Reser-
        vation, 197
    Tribal land, 88, 198, 200–4

Tribal sovereignty, 198–9, 201–4
  Ute tribal land, 203
  Yakama Nation Treaty of 1855, 200
Indonesia, 145
Interpol, 215*n*12
Interventionist foreign policy, 123
Involuntary servitude, 186. *See also* Slavery
Iowa, 118, 166*n*10
Iraq, 108, 134
Irish pauperism, 134
Iron Curtain, 47, 65. *See also* Cold War
Islamic world, 35–36
Isolation, 15, 89–91, 161
  "isolationism," 161
Italy, 79, 90*n*1, 106
  Northern Italy, 37

Jacksonians, 60, 60*n*16, 171
Japan, 69, 95, 106, 114, 119, 145–6
Jefferson, Thomas, 59
Jones, E.L., 39, 69
Judaism, 151–2
Juncker, Jean-Claude, 94

Kansas, 118, 166*n*10, 192
  Kansas Territory, 192
Kazakhstan, 128
Kehilot, 156
Kentucky, 118, 166, 168–70
Khrushchev, Nikita, 136
Kiev (Ukraine), 44, 129
Kirkpatrick Sale, 28, 28*n*1, 136
Knapp, Horace, 175
Knorr, Klaus, 113–14

Kohn, Richard, 164
Koyama, Mark, 36*n*2
Kraay, Aart, 93, 96–97
Krasner, Stephen, 97
Kuznets, Simon, 93

Landes, David, 39–40
Latin America, 91, 109, 161. *See also* The Americas
Latin Christendom, 36, 40*n*9
Latvia, 40
Lazarus, Emma, 191
Lemennicier, Bertrand, 126
Levellers, 162
Libertarian, Libertarianism, 7–8, 18, 22, 53, 63–64, 68, 78, 100, 162. *See also* Classical liberal
Liberty, 9, 22, 54*n*2, 58–59, 148, 164, 166. *See also* Freedom
Liechtenstein, 7, 90*n*1, 96, 108
Lincoln, Abraham, 169–70
Lithuania, 44, 74
"live and let live," 179
Localism, 19, 19*n*2, 22
  local autonomy, 16, 54, 77–78, 155, 208
  local control, 19*n*2, 22, 54*n*1, 61, 68, 171, 199, 213, 215*n*12
  local sovereignty, 19*n*2, 56, 204
Local conflicts over social policy, 12
Locally-based democracy, abandonment of, 148
London (England, UK), 121, 215
Lord Acton, 147–8
Lottieri, Carlo, 34, 34*n*6
Louisiana, 118, 183

Lousin, Ann, 193
Low Countries, 37. *See also* Belgium, Luxembourg, Netherlands
Loyalists, 75
Lübeck law, 156
Luxembourg, 90, 96, 108. *See also* Low countries

Madrid (Spain), 18
Magdeburg law, 156
Magoffin, Beriah, 168
Mailer, Norman, 63
Maine, 118, 174
Malta, Maltese, 67n10, 80, 83, 94
Malthusian trap, 36
Manhattan, 65
Marxism-inspired, 33
Maryland, 118, 183
Mason, George, 164–5
Massachusetts, 118, 168, 174, 182–3, 187, 189
    Massachusetts declaration of rights, 116
Mass democracy, 146, 149
Mearsheimers, John, 126, 130
Medicare, 213. *See also* Welfare state
Medicaid, 214. *See also* Welfare state
Mega-state, 6, 8, 27, 48, 65, 149, 211
Mexico, Mexican, 88
    Mexican American immigrants, 193
Michigan, 118, 166n10, 175, 192
    Michigan State Board of Health, 175
Microstates, 41, 70, 90, 92–93, 96

Middle Ages, 37–38, 146, 155
Middle East, 115
Minnesota, 109, 118, 171
Mises Institute, 13
Mississippi, 13, 171, 214
Missouri, 109, 118, 166n10
Mohr, James, 174
Mokyr, Joel, 41
Monaco, 108
Montana, 118, 166n10
Montesquieu, 7, 56–57
Montgomery Amendment, 171–2
Montgomery, Gillespie, 172
Moscow (Russia), 22, 70, 129n14
Mueller, John, 126–7
"myth of open borders," 190

National defense, 47, 107, 109
    Militia Act of 1903, 170
    National Defense Act of 1916, 171
    National Defense Authorization Act of 1987, 171
National Guard, 170–1
National election, 53, 179, 195
National Health Service, 179
National Forest lands, 199
National liberation, 73–76
    national liberation movements, 12
National Right to Life Committee, 173
"national will," 141
Nation-state, 32, 39, 65, 72, 74–75, 85, 109, 120, 146
Native American Party aka "Know-Nothings," 187
NATO, 107, 120

"Natural rights," 63
Nazism, 50
Nebraska, 32, 74, 118, 192
Netherlands, the, 38, 90n1, 119, 152. *See also* Low countries
    Dutch Republic, 16–17
Net wealth, 112
Neuman, Gerald, 181–2, 185–6, 190–2, 194
Nevada, 102, 118, 192
"The New Colossus," 191
New Hampshire, 118
New Jersey, 109, 118, 144
New Mexico, 87–88, 118
New York (city), 63, 65, 96
New York (state), 64–65, 101, 109, 118, 144, 146, 148, 167, 178, 182, 189, 209
New York v. Miln, 183
New Zealand, 48, 106
Nice (France), 78
Nigeria, 64, 75, 85
Non-majoritarian methods, 142
North America, 84, 119–20, 131. *See also* The Americas
    Confederation of North America, 60
    North American colonies, 182
North Carolina, 29, 109, 118, 166n10,
North Dakota, 69, 118
North, Douglass, 38, 69
North Korea, 51
Norway, 79, 81, 97, 106–7, 109
Nuclear weapon, nuclear warhead, nuclear arms, nuclear missiles, 125–35
    denuclearization, 129–31

nonnuclear states, 131
nuclear armed enemies, 125
nuclear armed states, nuclear power, nuclear force, 125, 128, 132, 135
nuclear arsenal, 49, 124, 126, 128, 130, 136
nuclear balance, nuclear parity, 132–3
nuclear conflict, nuclear war, nuclear strike, 49, 125, 128, 133–5
nuclear deterrence, 124, 126, 130, 133, 135
nuclear guarantees, 125
nuclear nonproliferation, 125–7
nuclear proliferation, 124–5

Ohio, 109, 118, 136, 166
Oklahoma, 118, 192, 198
"one man, one vote," 141–2, 142n1, 143–6
"oppressed minorities," 88
Oregon, 109, 118, 166n10, 192
    1857 state constitution, 186
Ozawa, Terutomo, 91

Pacifistic, 161
Papal States, 67n10, 79
Passenger Cases of 1849, 184
Pennsylvania, 109, 118, 166
"the people," 60n15, 84, 146, 148
The People's Liberation Army (PLA), 119, 121
Perkovich, George, 125
Pew Research Center, 178

Plebiscite, 48n10, 67, 67n10, 78, 78n1, 79–81

Poland, 71, 80, 107, 212

Polish-Lithuanian Commonwealth, 156

Politburo, 136

Political decentralization, 11–13, 20, 36, 141, 198, 200

Portugal, 39, 49

"Privatization" of Indian reservation lands, 197

Privileges and Immunities Clause, 197

Progressive Era, 177

Protectionism, 91

Protestant, 143–4. *See also* Catholic; Christian

Lutheran, 144

"quarantine" laws, 185

Quebec, 44, 64, 152

Quebecois nationalists, 75

Race relations, 11

Rachman, Gideon, 93

Raico, Ralph, 36, 40, 40n9, 56, 69

Raskin, Jamin, 193

Reagan, Leslie, 176–7

Red States of America, 118

Republicans, 185

Republic of Arcadia, 16

Republic of Geneva, 147

Republic of Ireland, 47

Retaliatory tariffs, 211

Rhine Valley, 78

Rhode Island, 118

Ricka, Franto, 94

Riga (Lithuania), 44

Rockwell, Lew, 22

Roe vs. Wade, 173–9

Roman Empire, 15

Western Roman Empire, 36

Romania, 49

Rome (Italy), 79

Rothbard, Murray, 22, 45, 54n1, 60n16, 63–66, 68–72, 74–75, 146n2, 162

Rousseau, Jean-Jacques, 147–9

Russia, 8, 49–50, 72–75, 84, 107–8, 114–15, 120–22, 128–9, 129n14, 130–1, 133–4, 156. *See also* Soviet Union

Russian Federation, 128, 130

Saar (French Protectorate), 80

Sale, Kirkpatrick, 28, 28n1, 136

Salerno, Joseph, 154

Sammons, Eric, 120

Sapolsky, Harvey, 125–7

Sardinia, 79

Saudi Arabia, 32

Savoy, 78

Schengen Agreement, 216

Schleswig question, 79

Scotland, 18, 44, 99–100, 105–10, 214–15. *See also* United Kingdom

Scottish independence, 105

Scottish voters, 18

Secession, 7–8, 11–12, 17, 47–48, 51, 59, 63–67, 67n10, 68, 72–77, 80–81, 83–84, 87–88, 99–102, 105, 108–09, 118, 120, 123–4, 127–8, 131, 136, 168–70, 204, 206, 216. *See also* secession and decentralization

Post-colonial secession movements, 12

Secession and decentralization, 11–12, 18, 21–22, 43, 47, 63, 68, 71, 89, 97, 103

"Secession is treason," 104

Secessionists, 18, 71, 74, 84, 99–100, 118, 120, 127–9, 168, 209

Secession movement, 11–12, 44, 47, 64, 74, 77–78, 84, 89, 99–100, 123, 128

Second World War, 49, 83, 124, 161

Security, 9, 17, 119, 164, 183

Self-government, 7–9, 22, 147, 154–6

Self-determination, 11, 22, 61, 66–68, 80, 84–88, 103, 103*n*3, 104, 154, 157

Semi-sovereign, 199

Serbia, 74. *See also* Yugoslavia

Slack, Michelle, 185, 190

Slater, Nick, 96

Slavery, 186. *See also* Involuntary servitude

Slovenia, 65, 67*n*10, 70, 73, 80–81. *See also* Yugoslavia

Small states, 7, 11, 22–23, 30–31, 40–41, 51, 68, 70, 91–97, 102, 132, 136. *See also* Micro-states

Sng, Tuan-Hwee, 36*n*2

Social Security, 213–14. *See also* Welfare state

Sokolski, Henry D., 124

South America, 20, 115. *See also* The Americas

South Carolina, 118, 185

South Dakota, 69, 118, 144, 166

South Korea, 145

South Sudan, 44

Sovereignty, 8, 83, 121, 168
    "sovereign nations," sovereign states, 199, 201, 12, 15, 20, 32, 40, 43, 63, 80–81, 84, 87

Soviet Union, 17, 43, 65, 67, 72, 76, 80, 84, 115, 126–8, 135–6. *See also* Russia
    Soviet Bloc, 71. *See also* Warsaw Pact

Spain, 18, 39, 90
    Spanish Empire, 17

Spolaore, Enrico, 92

Spooner, Lysander, 63

Stalin, Josef, 22

Standing army, 163–4, 167

State-building, 12, 17

State constitution, 32, 165–6, 191–2, 194–5. *See also* United States: Constitution

Statehood, 17, 103

State-level power, danger of, 209

States' rights, 61, 186

St. Bartholomew, 79

St. John, 79

St. Onge, Peter, 107

Storer and Heard ratio (of abortions per pregnancy), 175

Strong, George Templeton, 217

St. Thomas, 79

Subsidiarity, 18, 19*n*2

Sudetenland, 60

Sweden, 28, 67*n*10, 79, 131

Switzerland, 16, 90*n*1, 96, 107–9, 119, 136, 141, 143–4, 147–8, 155, 109
    Swiss confederation, 143

Swiss Council of States, 142
Swiss method of "double majority," 142–3

Ten-Day War, 67n10, 72, 80
Tennessee, 118, 187
Territoriality, 8
"territorial integrity," 72, 74, 87–88, 130
Texas, 109, 118, 148, 179, 202, 209
Third Reich, 80
Thorhallsson, Baldur, 131
Tilly, Charles, 45
Tokyo (Japan), 16
Trade, 35, 37, 90–92, 91–92n3, 93, 96, 106–7, 121
    Commercium et pax (trade and peace)
    Free trade, 8, 32, 70, 145. See also Free market
    Legal trade, 33
    Smuggling, 33
    Trade barriers, 42, 68, 89, 95, 97, 107
Transfer payments, 106, 213
Treaty of Prague, 79
Trump, Donald, 99, 136, 198
Tse Tung, Mao, 108
Tshombe, Moise, 64
Turkish Cyprus, 64
Tyler, John, 190–1

Ukraine, 44, 67n10, 80, 126, 128–9, 129n14, n15, 130
Unification processes, 8
    Unificationists, 34n6
Unionists, 170

United Kingdom, 18, 48, 67n10, 105, 108, 115, 211, 216. See also Brexit; British state; England; Great Britain; Scotland.
    House of Commons, 142
United Nations, 84, 87
United States, 16, 20, 28–29, 32, 34–35, 41, 43, 47, 61, 63, 65, 77, 79, 83, 87–88, 100–102, 107, 109, 111–12, 115, 117–21, 123–4, 129–31, 136, 141, 145, 161, 163–4, 167–71, 175, 181–2, 187–8, 190, 192–5, 199, 203, 206, 209, 212–14, 216. See also American Revolution
    American Southwest, 87
    Civil War, 168, 188, 192, 216
    Congress, 143, 200
    Constitutional convention, 164
    Declaration of Independence, 59, 84, 163
    Electoral College system, 142
    House of Representatives, 142n1
    Northeastern states, 188–9
    The Northern side, the North, 169–70
    Postal Service, 176
    President, 134, 143, 167–8, 171, 177, 207–8
    Secretary of War, 167
    Senate, 141–2
    Southern States, the South, 65, 101, 107, 168–70, 185
    Supreme Court, 68, 142n1, 171, 173, 177–8, 194, 199–200
United States Constitution, 60, 163, 165, 167–171, 179, 182,

185*n*11, 187, 192, 194–5, 206.
See also Articles of Confederation
  American constitutional law,
    11–12
  Bill of Rights, 60, 60*n*15
  Fourteenth Amendment,
    60*n*15
  Second Amendment, 163
  Tenth Amendment, 60*n*15, 68
United States of Europe, 216
United States of East Asia, 145
Universalism vs. localism, 22
Universal rights, locally enforced,
  19, 22
"unoccupied" lands, 199
"unorganized militia," 166
Utah, 118, 146

Va'ad Arba' Aratzot, 156
van Creveld, Martin, 46
Venaissin, Comtat, 78
Venezuela, 33
Venice (Italy), 44
Vermont, 108, 118, 167
Vietnam, 145
Virginia, 29, 118, 164–5, 166*n*10
  Virginia ratifying convention,
    164–5
"virtue signaling," 84
von Bismarck, Otto, 84
von Mises, Ludwig, 50*n*13, 66, 78,
  154
Vorarlberg, 79–80

Wal-Mart, 29, 29*n*3
Waltz, Kenneth, 124–7, 132–6
Wambaugh, Sarah, 67*n*11, 78*n*1

War of 1812, 121, 167
Warsaw Pact, 71. *See also* Soviet
  bloc
Wars on Terror, 108
Washington, DC, 35, 42, 99, 170,
  217
Washington (state), 118, 192, 200
  *Washington State Dept. of
    Licensing v. Cougar Den, Inc.*,
    200
Welfare state, 46, 99, 214, 214*n*8.
  See also Medicaid; Medicare;
  Social Security
West Virginia, 118, 214*n*8
White House, 214
"will of the people," 148
Wisconsin, 118, 192, 194
  1848 state constitution, 192
  Wisconsin Supreme Court,
    194
Woodbury, Levi, 192
World Bank, 97, 108
Wyoming, 118, 166*n*10, 192,
  199–200

Yassky, David, 165
Yerevan (Armenia), 44
Yugoslavia, 47, 67*n*10, 72–74, 80.
  See also Bosnia-Herzegovina,
  Serbia, Slovenia
Yugoslav Wars, 80

Znamenski, Andrei, 40–41*n*9